LEADERSHIP: FROM TELESCOPE TO MICROSCOPE

LEADERSHIP ARTICLES FROM 'TOP VOICE ON LINKEDIN'

PROF DR AJIT PATIL

Copyright © Prof Dr Ajit Patil
All Rights Reserved.

When she got married she was just 19. She is from the most respected Bhosale family, Chattrapati Shivaji Maharaj's lineage. She has a fighter's DNA and blue blood. When she got married, she started working at that tender age. I was born when she was 20 and at 22 my younger brother, Jayant, was born. She was sterilized immediately. Now I just can't imagine that.

My mother worked very hard. She used to go to morning college, 7.30 AM to 11 AM then worked till late evening. For 7 days a month night shifts, from 10 PM till 7 AM. My brother and I used to be alone at home. We were not even 10. She raised two sons with no support from any relative. For many years my father used to work as a professor in different cities. She had to manage everything alone with two sons. She completed graduation, completed master's, and then a bachelor's in education. She studied for 7 long years after having kids & while working. She secured BA; MA; B Ed degrees. I am so proud of what she did, how she did and under what circumstances she did it. I owe her a lot.

In the 1960s and 70s, she had to walk everywhere, in Solapur, since there wasn't public transport and she couldn't ride a bicycle. Her job required her to stand for 8 hours. She developed varicose veins. Now at 78, she had to be operated on for both knee replacements. I told her not to bother anyone. I went to Pune. I took good care of her, stay there with her for a few days and then come back only after she walked firmly. I served her alone. This was just a partial interest repayment on her deposit.... I can't repay her debt in my life. Just before the pandemic, I took her to Switzerland with my father, wife, and daughter. That was the golden period in her life. Then we went to America and had quality family time with Jayant, Anu, and Nishat, in Atlanta. She stayed back with Jayant for 2 more months. She was meeting him after 8 years. I am not fair like her (in complexion) but I want to be fair to my mother. God blessed her with sharp features and ever smiling face. At my wedding, she was looking like my elder sister. People from my wife's side thought she was my father's second wife and hence looked much younger. Even today, my father looks 82 but she looks 65. Though there is just a 3- year gap in their age.

I realized the greatest debt in the world is the debt of milk. Lucky are those who get the opportunity to serve that debt though they can't repay it. She has had her quota of pains. Now I want to soak her pain in my love, that is the only sedative a mother has, her son's love.

This book is dedicated to my mother, Vandana.......

Contents

Contents

Prof Dr. Ajit Patil's Profile

Prof Dr Ajit Patil is an accomplished management professional, erudite Management Consultant and Coach, Consummate academician, prolific writer, a celebrated professor of Marketing and Retailing, and a meticulous researcher. He is a Production Engineer with an MBA in Marketing from Sydenham Institute of Management Studies, University of Mumbai. He is awarded a PhD in Marketing Management (Retailing) by Pune University.

He has been associated with the industry for over 30 years. He has worked at the senior management level in international and domestic sales and Marketing after starting his career in manufacturing. He has been teaching Sales/Marketing and Retailing subjects to MBA students in India and overseas for 18 years.

He is awarded "**Top-75 influential Marketing Professors in the World**" in 2020. He is actively involved in consultancy. As a Management Consultant, Adviser and Coach he provides advice on Business Strategy, Marketing Planning, and Sales Management to companies and retailers.

He is a known writer and was awarded the 'Top Voice on LinkedIn" in 2017. Case Studies written by him have won national and international awards. He has presented them at international conferences in the USA and India. Few of his case studies are published in international journals.

He has conducted Management Development Programmes and In-Company training Programmes for Companies like Indian Oil Ltd, Indian Postal Services, Steel Authority of India, Padmakshi Financials, Brenntag India Ltd, Polygel Industries, etc. He regularly conducts Sales Training Programmes for the field staff, sales managers, and channel partners. He has taught in Faculty Development Programmes on Case Study teaching and writing. His 6 books are published. Some of them are textbooks for MBA/ MMS students at the University of Mumbai and Pune University.

He has travelled extensively in the USA, UK, Germany, France, Netherlands, Belgium, China, Fiji, Samoa and Tonga for work, research and teaching. He has done extensive proprietary post-doctoral research on the global retailers in the USA, China, Europe and Hong Kong besides the study of the Indian retail sector as a part of his Ph D.

He is a member of the American Marketing Association (AMA) and North American Case Research Association (NACRA) which are associations of marketing professionals and management professors, respectively, based in America.

Mobile: +91 9819943643

e-mail: ajitpatilmumbai@yahoo.co.in

LinkedIn Profile:

https://www.linkedin.com/in/prof-dr-ajit-patil-mumbai-india-56281b1a/

Thane, India.

21 August 2022

Prologue

This book explains the following topics: -

1. **Grooming Leaders at Home:** -Family-managed businesses are very particular about imparting leadership to their young generation. They start grooming the leaders at home during the early stages of life. Usually, fathers take ownership of grooming the emerging leaders in the family. Fathers are tough and possessive. They have their own methods and tools. Aditya Birla and Dhirubhai were such fathers who developed exemplary leaders. How did they groom leaders at home? How should the upbringing of our children be done if we want them to be leaders of the future? What is our role as a parent?

2. **Leaders Don't Negotiate:** - People can't negotiate with leaders. They demand, request, and pursue leaders for their gains but leaders don't negotiate. Why? How do leaders push their agenda forward without negotiations? Why do they not believe in the negotiations?

3. **Leading Sung and Unsung Heroes:** -Organizations are built by the contributions made by the heroes and the sacrifices made by the unsung heroes. Leaders themselves are sung heroes though they would love to remain otherwise. They stand with the support of unsung heroes. How do leaders create these sung and unsung heroes? How do they create leaders?

4. **Why are Leaders Fearless?:** - Most of us generate self-inflicting fears. These fears are usually because of unawareness rather than uncertainties. One of the most common qualities among leaders is that they are fearless. Leaders educate themselves to fight against their fears. The fearlessness makes them dare to walk firmly towards the mission. Leaders have extra energy because they conserve it rather than wasting it on fears.

5. **Leaders: At Peace With Themselves:** - The leaders are always at peace with themselves. They know what they can do and what they can't. Leaders clearly know their mission, their path, the resources they need, and also how to get those resources. Leaders are not just obsessed with the mission but they also cherish their journey towards the mission. Leaders have the capability to understand the milestones in the journey. Those milestones ensure that they are on the right path. They know very

well when to accelerate and also how to slow down.

6. **Silence: A Leader's Wisdom:** - Great leaders use words like money and transactions like ATM machines, and the environment with only bare minimum words. They want people to tell them problems in the way the leader wants to listen. long stories are not welcomed by them. Many people go to a leader with the same problems hence he is usually aware of the background and the issue. That is the reason why the leader wants people to skip an introduction and come straight to the point. As a professional grow in the organization and moves up the ladder he realizes, 'Less is more. For him, words are an important resource. He hardly or sparingly uses it. How do they do it?

7. **Teaching Leaders Their Business:** - I started teaching MBA students ever since my daughter, Supriya, was in school. She used to wonder, whom did I teach? What did I teach? Probably those were the most difficult question posed to a management professor. I ask myself do I teach Marketing? or Retailing or Sales? Why do I go to my class? What is one thing that I do in my class? Over a period of time, when she grew up, I developed an answer.

8. **Leader: Changing Potential Energy to Kinetic:** - Managers are 'professionals' and leaders are 'entrepreneurs'. What is the difference? what are those rare leadership qualities? What makes the leader outstanding, rather standout?

9. **Why Do Men On Mission Deliver?:** - We identify a few people as crazy people. Their craze is the mission they chase. Crazy people write history. Why do these crazy people deliver the result? Why do they achieve what others don't? What is the source of their energy? What are their tools? What are their methods? They are the men on a mission. (The term is used for both genders)

10. **Leadership Style: Online or Offline:** - Is leading from the front the only best strategy? To what extent does the physical presence of the leader matter? Is it a must? Can the leader lead from the war room or a boardroom? I call leading from the front 'Online leadership' and leading from the boardroom or the war room 'leading in Absentia' or 'Offline Leadership'.

11. **Leading Flat Organizations:** - Today, the younger organizations prefer flat organization structures. Are they only taking the lopsided view? What are the challenges involved in leading flat organizations? Leading multi-layered organizations certainly poses a challenge. But leading a flat

organization is not easy either. A flat organization can exert power only if it is led by a powerful leader. Such a leader has to be ambidextrous. He is a master of the art of delegation. He inspires his team with a mission. His team has the burning desire to succeed. They are emotionally connected to each other. They have to be 'hands-on' and push each other up. Sharing and caring are their strengths. Flat organizations have to be process driven but they encarve short-cuts very well. Members of the flat organization are high on conceptual skills. They create competitive advantages by looking at the total picture. They would never lose woods for trees. Such flat organizations have lesser inertia, higher agility, and better customer centricity.

12. **Status Quo Leadership:** - Under some special situations, a few managers, who are followers, are appointed as leaders. They know self-limitations, for sure. Such 'nominated leaders' always fear change and they struggle to maintain the status quo. They know very well that they can be drowned in change. Status quo leaders always project that their organization has reached its peak.

13. **Quasi Leadership:** - 'Quasi-leaders look like leaders. They have many features of leaders but for a few critical ones. Mission, chemistry with the team, uniqueness of characters like glamour and grace, caliber and talent, support of the gut, and public relation (PR) skills could be the missing links between quasi-leaders and leaders. Quasi-leaders rise to leadership stature because they are at right the right place at the right time. They become leaders after some great leaders who are too possessive and don't do succession planning. Some leaders initially appear like quasi-leaders but eventually mature as roaring tigers. How do such quasi-leaders lead? What legacy do they leave and how to deal with such leaders if you are their followers?

14. **Training the Traits:** - When we lose important battles against our competition despite giving our 100%, then remember that traits played the difference. For the final attack, we need to set our team as per their traits, train them well, and make them develop their own software.

15. **From Crown to Captaincy- Transforming Leadership Game:** -As the jobs are transforming into careers, boundaries between the workplace and home are vanishing. Offices are getting embedded in homes as the 'work from home' concept propagates. Millennials, the young leaders in their 30s (born after the year 1980) are changing the leadership game. These young leaders are keeping the crown aside and wearing

the captaincy cap. The leaders are evolving as captains. An increasing number of corporate leaders are looking at leadership as a responsibility rather than a position.

16. **From Deputy to Chief- Journey of Thousand Miles:** - Becoming the Deputy need not be the last step toward the chief's chair. Why do most of the deputies exhaust their stamina and fail to move on to the top slot? Do they lack some of the leadership skills required by the chief? Many times the deputy is selected on parameters that are radically different from the parameters necessary for the chief's position.

17. **Succeeding Success - A Leadership Challenge:** - Great leaders electrify their chairs. Their successor finds it difficult to sit on such an electric chair. They feel the strong current in that chair. We compare the personality of such tall leaders with the new incumbent. Most of the time such comparison is unfair. We compare the character of these great leaders after they achieve success, with the new leaders who are just beginning their tenure. The successor has to manage these expectations which is a great challenge.

18. **Leadership: A skyscraper TightRope Walk:** - Leadership is like walking on a tight rope hung between two towers that are 110 floors high. The Hollywood movie, 'The walk' highlights the qualities of leadership required in order to achieve any mega success, be it personal or organizational.

19. **Alert and Alive Leadership:** - Businesses are facing a macro-environment that is highly fluid requiring dynamic strategic planning. The leadership has to be alert and alive. Their reactions should be like reflexes, quick & accurate. Competitors can catch you on the wrong foot if they find you napping. The long-term plan is becoming more of a hurdle than a tool that enables growth. Gone are the days when the governments used to prepare a five-year plan and swear by it. Even the Government of India has abolished the planning commission. Leaders are looking for flexibility in planning. In fact, the alert and alive customers demand alive brands and alert marketers.

20. **Alignment - The Art of Agreement:** - Migrating birds have developed a technique to fly with less energy so they can fly hundreds of miles. This technic is alignment. Leaders can train their teams to get aligned. This can save organizational resources which are wasted in overcoming internal resistance. Alignment can bring synergy and optimize organizational resources. Alignment gets the organization to cruise in

auto mode.

21. **Gut Feel - Leader's Third Eye:-** Leaders have better gut feeling management. Many leaders first develop gut and then search for the evidence, before making decisions. Leaders have the courage to follow their gut feeling. They know the risk involved with gut-based decision-making, but still, they dare it. Sometimes they are compelled to take the risk due to their role in the team.

22. **Leveraging: A Core Leadership Skill: -** Leveraging is using a lever, which is a type of tool, to reduce the efforts required to lift a load. It is easier to lift the heavier object using a lever rather than trying to lift it directly. In simple words leveraging is getting much more as an output compared to the input. This happens due to some factors or tools. Identifying such factors and devising such tools, to gain higher output, is the leveraging skill. Leadership has to identify the strengths/advantages of their organization, scale them up and leverage them to gain industry leadership.

23. **Managing Access: Lesson From History: -** Most leaders are busy people. Time is the most scarce resource for them. They can't spare time for everybody who demands their time. They have to be choosy. Access to the leader is a privilege. I have seen many people making their careers out of such access. Some use it responsibly, some use it sparingly but most of them overuse it and even misuse it. This article is about managing such privileged access to power. If not handled properly, access can even ruin the leadership. Human history offers many examples and modern-day management leaders must draw their lessons from those stories.

24. **Gaining By Giving: A Leadership Trait: -** Leadership is about giving. Leaders give wealth, leaders give career, leaders give purpose to life, and leaders give hope. Leaders give many things to many people. Great leaders sense the needs of their people and give them much more than their greed. They give & enjoy the joy of giving. However, they push their mission ahead while they are busy giving. The main purpose of giving is to extract energy from the people for the mission.

25. **Managing Glamour - A Leadership Challenge: -** Political and corporate leaders are blessed with glamour. Their greatness lies in their ability to provide energy from their aura to their team. The glittering aura lightens up their journey toward their mission. Glamorous leaders are required to take initiative in making collaborative efforts. Handling glamour

determines the taste of the leadership. Some exploit it for personal gain, they create wealth. Others leverage it for humanity. They build a network and make it work for their mission. The causes behind such leveraging determine the height of the leadership.

26. **Leader's Art of Super Human Management:** - As machines replaced labor, the 'Personnel department' transformed into Human Relationship Management (HRM) department. With the emergence of the service economy, the 'high tech & high touch' approach became important. Talent got prominence. Attracting, retaining, and managing talent became the critical HRM activity. Talent Management is not just the modern avatar of HRM but there is more to it. It deals with managing the super-human, Super-Human Relationship Management (SHRM).

27. **Recruitment - Missing a Shot:** - Why do Goldman Sachs and Tata Administrative Services (TAS) conduct seven rounds of interviews during the recruitment process? What are they looking for? What do they access? How do they access it? Why are they so obsessed with eliminating the 'black sheep'? An insight into the great leaders' minds and their approach to selecting their team.

28. **Why Do Leaders Get up?:** - People were shocked when Jack Ma stepped down as Chairman of the board of Alibaba by handing over the management function to Daniel Zhang. They were surprised to see Jack getting up and getting out of the management when Alibaba locked horns with Amazon. Jack understood the leadership game better. He learnt it from the veterans like Warren Buffet, Robson Walton, and Bill Gates. They also handed over the management to their successors, whom they groomed, and preferred to remain owners. They understood the leadership role conceptually.

29. **The Power of Delegation:** - Delegation is not just passing on the authority, it means enabling somebody to act. It is the method by which you acknowledge the potential of your subordinates and show trust in their competencies. It is the way to pass on the positive message and feelings about people. It is the process by which you help people to perform their jobs. People can feel the leadership better when the leaders delegate their authority to their people. Delegation develops your followers as the leader grows. The delegation also develops autonomy by empowering the employees. The team dynamics develop The 'Hands On' attitude of the team. It helps to make the organization 'Customer Centric'.

30. **Leading: From Maximumto Optimum Mindset:** - In the rat race for maximizing profits and sales, companies forget the flip side and the damages get created. Wise leaders focus on identifying the interests of all the stakeholders.

31. **Flexing Reflexes - The Ultimate Leadership Skill:** - Decision-making on reflexes is an important skill in leadership and management. It can be developed with a lot of training and practice. The leaders should facilitate their employees in such a decision-making process. Wherein the employees get trained and empowered to make spontaneous decisions in response to the business stimuli. Decision-making on reflexes, with lightning speed, will mark successful organizations.

32. **No Does Not Mean Never:** - It is important to learn to say and also to receive 'No' in life. How and when to say No is an art. Handling No is a part of wisdom. No may not be a hurdle. It can be a foundation of innovation.

33. **Political Leadership:** - Corporate leadership certainly has its own set of challenges but Political leadership offers higher rigor, risk, and challenges. Politicians have to deal with many more variables, stakeholders, and complex situations. They have to hit harder targets. Political leadership has to deal with running and intermittently invisible targets. The worst part of a political career is not having formal training. This article discusses these challenges. (Published on LinkedIn on 8 July 2017.

34. **Learning to Compete in the Unfair Environment:** - Leaders know that there is no point in complaining about the unfair environment. In every Market, there will be a few competitors who will have certain unfair advantages. The leadership challenge is how to nullify them.

35. **I Don't Agree But I Accept:** - Concludingbrainstorming sessions are always difficult. Initially, we love the differences that emerge out of discussions but then the going gets tough when people stick to their viewsand& don't budge. Some differences are impossible to bridge. What should be done in such cases?

36. **Black is not the opposite of white:** - We have a tendency to compare two things and stamp them. This develops prejudice. We unnecessarily treat certain things as opposite, like Black and White. Such prejudice blocks us from looking at the world objectively. Leaders have to develop their perspective to see things as different rather than bad or opposite in nature.

37. **The Second Opinion:** - When we are facing a grave situation, physical, mental, or otherwise, we seek the opinions and advice of experts in the respective field. Sometimes we find it difficult to digest that opinion or advice. We seek advice from another expert. This second opinion either confirms the first or goes against it. Leaders handle this process and their advice well.

38. **Leadership by Partnership:** - In modern organizations, leadership is evolving. There could be different leaders for different goals depending upon the nature of the goal and the expertise available. Some organizations are testing leadership by rotation so that many people will get benefits and the conceptual skills, cooperation, and coordination within the team improve.

39. **Collaborating While Competing:** - Rivalry isn't always bad. It keeps the leadership on toes. But collaboration with the rival is also necessary. The article discusses how to compete but still collaborate.

CHAPTER ONE

Gaining by Giving: A Leadership Trait

eadership is about giving. Leaders give wealth, leaders give career, leaders give purpose to life, and leaders give hope. Leaders give many things to many people. Great leaders sense the needs of their people and give them much more than their greed. They give and enjoy the joy of giving. However, they push their mission ahead while they are busy giving. The main purpose of giving is to extract energy from the people for the mission. (Published on LinkedIn on 24 February 2018. Got 400 Likes; 29 Comments and 68 Shares).

> *"Nobody follows a person who takes. People follow a leader who gives, hence giving is an important leadership trait."*

How are leaders conceived? My students ask me what is the test of leadership. How do you know that you are getting transformed from a follower to a leader? I tell them, they would start getting into the leader's position when they start giving more than they take. The leader gives 60 & takes 40. As the leader grows, the ratio of giving to taking grows, 65-35, 70-30, 75-25, 80-20, etc.

Finally, a leader *starts taking only the energies of people for his mission.*

> *"When the thoughts of giving more to people come to your mind, be assured that you are becoming a leader."*

Leaders, like kids, know the power of demonstrating their affection. They are good at showering their love. Kids know how to delight an angry mother. They kiss her on the cheek and their mother melts. When a leader smiles at them, puts an arm around their shoulders, or shakes their hands, the follower gets charged. Shaking hands or taking a selfie is a lifetime experience for the followers. They relish those memories & carry those snaps like a medal.

> *"Giving is an important attitude of the leader. Leaders are in the business of giving."*

Giving Something to Everybody They develop corporations that create the 'Wow' factor among their customers by giving them much more than what customers pay for. Great leaders give dividends and bonus shares to their investors. They are aware of the trust shown by the investors in their leadership & make efforts to stay up to the expectations of the investors. Leaders provide prosperity to their channel partners. They have a sense of responsibility towards the channel partners who get associated with them in serving the customers. The great leaders identify the fair share of investors and other business associates like suppliers, dealers, etc. in their growth & suitably compensate them by giving the right financial rewards.

"Great leaders master the art of giving. They are very creative. They understand what can be priceless for the other person."

They know money is not the only thing people expect from them. They realize the hunger of their people for their love and affection. Leaders cherish the priceless emotions that they generate by giving. Great leaders are extremely sensitive people. They have high Emotional Intelligence. Their high EQ gives them a great ability to empathize with their people. They visualize the ecstasy which the other person gets after the leader gifts them something. Great leaders leverage the power of money but they know that money can't do everything. The leaders give a rewarding career, stability, and financial benefits to their employees.

"Great leaders don't attach any danglers or riders to their givings."

How do Leaders Grow? The leader holds the top position in the team so from where would his growth come? The leader grows by three things. First, the growth of the leader depends on his mission. The broader the base of the followers the taller the leader grows. The wider he inflicts his mission, the faster he grows. How more and more people join his mission and contribute their energies to it, defines the success and height of the leader. The second, test of a leader is how fast & how close he takes the team to the mission. Achieving a mission really takes a long time. A leader is called successful when he closes into the mission faster. Lastly, the higher the hope he raises, the higher he grows. The interim progress helps to raise hopes. The leader can make his base broader, and close to the mission faster only when he develops an attitude of 'giving'. The more & more leader gives, the more and more expectations grow. More and more people start expecting more & more things from the leader. It sets off the chain of hope. This chain of hope binds followers to the leaders & the team pulls the mission with the chain of hope.

Source of the fame There are many reasons why leaders get their fame. Broader the base of their leadership larger the aura they get. It also works another way round. Brighter the aura stronger the base of the leadership. They shine because of their aura & attract followers. Their people stay with them because of their attitude and skill of giving.

"Great leaders get their aura and glamour from their power to give."

How do they give what they give? Different leaders follow different ways of giving. The leader sets an organization's culture by adopting a typical way. Some leaders chose to give secretively while others love giving publicly. They might give prizes in cash or kind or show a kind gesture. I have seen many leaders wanting to give pleasant surprises to their people. They love the spontaneity of the positive emotions when they gift something to somebody. Some leaders give surprises but secretively. They hate to do it publicly. They feel it is a cheap display of feelings. But some leaders create energy by gifting publicly. They know that they can't hide appreciation for the person from others. Sooner or later everybody gets to know about it and then others feel bad and misread the intentions. In such a case the leader prefers to give openly. He appreciates an achievement publicly, generates satisfaction among achievers, sends a positive message, and generates sibling rivalry through peer pressure.

Expectations Management is the most critical job of the leader. He has to manage the expectations of people within the organization and also the people outside. Managing the people outside the organization provides a social status to the leader and develops the corporate brand.

"Managing expectations becomes the key job of the leader. The longer he manages expectations the longer he stays in control and the longer his people stay with him."

Great leaders have great challenges. Every mouth that opens to speak, requests for something. Every eye contact he makes, asks something. Every phone call, every personal visit, and every email demands something from the leader. The leader has to learn to manage such situations.

"Unfulfilled expectations of the team members can be more dangerous than competitive threats."

Ordinary leaders get pissed off due to such pressure of expectations. They succumb to the pressure & tend to manhandle it. Unfulfilled expectations have the power to turn friends into foes. It can breed vengeance. Such employees try to harm the leader by harming the organizational interest. It can backfire strongly and can damage.

"Great leaders say 'yes' promptly and handle 'no' gracefully."

Great leaders know that the delay in saying 'yes' can spoil the impact it can create. People equate delayed 'yes' to 'no'. Leaders are genuine people and feel bad when they can't give something to somebody

"Even a fool can say 'yes' but it requires a man of wisdom to say 'no'."

In a nutshell, great leaders understand the 'power of giving'. It comes naturally to them. They take less and give much more. They actively look for an opportunity to give something to someone. They are masters of knowing who wants what. People keep asking them for many things. They are careful while saying 'no'. The follower gets transformed into a leader when he learns the art of giving. The giving attitude provides an aura to the leader. 'Giving' provides glamour. It is an important trait that helps the leader in fulfilling the mission.

CHAPTER TWO

Grooming Leaders at Home

Family-managed businesses are very particular about imparting leadership to their young generation. They start grooming the leaders at home during the early stages of life. Usually, fathers take ownership of grooming the emerging leaders in the family. Fathers are tough and possessive. They have their own methods and tools. Aditya Birla and Dhirubhai were such fathers who developed exemplary leaders. How did they groom leaders at home? How should the upbringing of our children be done if we want them to be the leaders of the future? What is our role as a parent? (Published on LinkedIn on 28 Feb 2019. Got 3008 Likes; 116 Comments and 199 Shares)

"Business families don't just search for emerging talent, they produce it at home."

For the leaders of family-managed businesses, home is the b-school. They learn life lessons at home. They also have role models at home. Usually, fathers are the 'talent managers', due to obvious reasons, while mothers focus on developing emotional intelligence. Grandfathers are revered as role models while the grandmothers generate human bonds and develop social skills. For many business scions, fathers and uncles are the 'go-to men' for domain knowledge and for crisis management, a mother is a soft-skill trainer and the grandparents are teachers who nurture ethics and family values.

"Fathers teach in the office, mother on the dinning table, grand father on the lap and grandmother through bedtime stories."

Sibling Rivalry Siblings and cousins not only provide benchmarks for performance measurement but also put peer pressure by raising performance standards through their achievements. The higher the sibling rivalry the higher the performance. They introduce healthy competition and teach how to compete while you cooperate with each other. Business scions develop lobbying skills while outfoxing other kids.

Safety Net The extended family lays the support net which helps while getting into new businesses and ventures. They provide psychological support and also support in trade relationships. Great leaders like Aditya Birla realized that just a leadership DNA, management education, and inheritance weren't enough for their next generation to succeed in the Indian business environment. G D Birla laid the foundation, Aditya Birla created the Birla empire, and Kumarmangalam gave it a global scale and transformed a Marwari company into a professional company. Kumarmangalam Birla took over as the Chairman of the Aditya Birla Group in 1995, at the age of 28, following the death of his father. During his tenure as chairman, the group's annual turnover increased from US$3.33 Billion in 1995 to US$41 billion in 2015. Every Birla generation, with its unique leadership style, created its footprints. They added value and led the company for life.

"Business families have core values, business models and philosophy. These assets are passed on from generations to generations."

Understanding inheritance and legacy Business families have a deep understanding of inheritance, they know how to create and maintain the legacy. The family-managed businesses have their own core competencies which have been developed over the years. The leadership style and scale change from leader to leader but these core competencies shared values and collective wisdom remain the same. Different business communities in India have different business philosophies and business models. Marwaris, Gujrathis, Kachis, Sindhis, Banias, Chetiyars, Boharis, and Punjabis differ from each other in these parameters and preferences. These things are deeply rooted because they form a part of childhood.

"In 'Family Managed Businesses', fathers added value by providing required exposure, training and hand-holding in formative years."

In the Birla family, fathers spent a lot of time with their children, educated them well, and provided them with the required exposure at right time. They ensured that their next generation would go through the rigor, labor, and pains of development. Mr. Aditya Birla did it by making his son, Kumarmangalam pursues a professional degree, in CA, alongside his under-graduation degree, B Com. Kumarmangalam admits today, that this decision was the best decision imposed upon him by his father. The academic pressure crushed him hard but he came out as a winner with enhanced stamina and persistence. It increased his tenacity and ability to perform under huge pressure and expectations. Such upbringing is Kumarmangangalm Birla's real wealth. his challenge is how he takes this legacy forward as a father.

"Bill Gates used to drive and drop his daughter to school himself in the morning, before reaching office, spending 45 minutes."

Bill Gates' daughter's school was not on his way to his office but was in the opposite direction. His wife was reluctant to drive 30 minutes in either direction because she had to take care of 2 more kids at home. Bill offered to help her and used to drop his daughter happily at her school at least 2 days a week. He took out time from his busy schedule to be with his daughter. They discussed many things, with his daughter on the way while driving the car. It was a part of her upbringing. Bill Gates brought a social change by demonstrating how responsible a father he was. Listen to his wife Melinda gates interview on YouTube telling more about this.

> *"Great leaders are great fathers, they teach through their deeds and become heroes of their kids too."*

Great leaders take out the time for their kids rather than giving any excuses. It is their investment in the future of their company and securing the future of their mission. Such investment pays off. Great leaders shoulder their social responsibility of bringing up socially responsible kids and emerging leaders. They treat fatherhood as a societal responsibility and create role models for society by raising the bar for other fathers. Ajay Piramal had to join the family business immediately after his MBA (MMS) from Jamnalal Bajaj (JBIMS) in Mumbai. The untimely and sad demise of his beloved elder brother, Ashok, passed on the leadership baton at a very young age. His upbringing helped Ajay Piramal to become what he is today.

> *"Great leaders do get certain unfair advantages but they have to face a lot more unfair expectations."*

Leaders of family-managed businesses are measured against huge benchmarks. They have to fight against the law of averages which predicts their performance because they are the sons of successful fathers and grandfathers. Ambanis, Singhanias, Piramals, Birlas, and other family-managed businesses have to maintain this tradition if India has to become a superpower. Outliers in their family can put their business empire in danger.

> *"Leadership comes as inheritance only when the person develops an ability to add value."*

This explains the mega success of the industry leaders from family-managed businesses like Mukesh Ambani, Kumar Mangalam Birla, and his father, Rahul Bajaj, Robson Walton, etc. The deficit on this account can put the person in difficulty. The tenure of the leadership depends on their ability to keep themselves up-to-date and relevant by adding value. The formal position becomes redundant for them.

> *"The best investment in the world is investing time in your children. Get into their world and help them in getting into the real world."*

Great political leaders also invest time in their children. Pandit Nehru wrote beautiful letters to Indira from prison. Xi Zing-ping used to take his daughter on bicycle rides. Emerging leaders, even from the political parties, must learn this. The leadership future of promising Indian leaders like Priyanka Gandhi, Akhilesh Yadav, Stalin, Supriya Sule, and Praniti Shinde depends on their ability to add value.

> *"The child of the leader who develops the ability to contribute becomes the 'leadership heir' rather than a legal heir. Struggling business and political scions lack this ability hence get rejected in spite of the leader's efforts to pass-on the inheritance."*

Cursing own profession at the dining table Some parents seek my advice to convince their children to get into their professions but kids don't want to do that. Parents feel they are fools. I educate parents and tell them that they are the source. They keep cursing their profession on the dining table or in the drawing hall discussions. Kids listen to it carefully and form their opinions against that profession.

> *"Business families teach their kids the world is same everywhere, seeking opportunities is important than just complaining."*

Developing Attitudes B schools impart knowledge, experience develops skills. Business families focus on developing the right attitudes to make their next generation 'Business ready'. Business families provide training to their kids on how to compete in the unfair world. They provide training to mold the environment rather than looking at it as a hurdle. They also develop an attitude to look at the half glass full rather than looking another way round. The 'On-Off' switch gets fitted which becomes useful to lead happy family life while working under huge pressure in the business.

Our Story Our only daughter Supriya always makes us very proud parents. She secured Maharashtra Governments' high school scholarship, secured 96% in SSC (10th-grade board) exams, and 90% in the 12th-grade exam in Commerce. In 2016, she secured the Gold Medal from Mr. Mukesh Ambani, during convocation for securing the first rank in the University of Mumbai undergraduate degree, Bachelor of Commerce, B Com in 2016. She was selected for an internship in a very tough selection process, by the Swiss Bank and did her internship at Credit Suisse Asia Pacific office in Hong Kong, China. It was a proud moment to see her sitting on the 99th floor of the 107 storied tallest building in Hong Kong which is the commercial capital of Asia. Now she works with the Tata Group company, Tata Capital. She is identified as the 'Emerging Leader' at just 23 years of age. She scored 730 marks on her GMAT score which can take her to Harvard or Wharton business school for sure. Her strong bond with the socially committed Tata group made her stay back. She is happily joining Tatas in their mission to make India an economic superpower.

My wife, Arti, (the Managing Director of the reputed bank in Mumbai), and I realized Supriya's leadership talent at an early age. We tried very hard to give her maximum time. Her mother who was an exceptionally good student in her school days, used to take care of Supriya's studies while I was touring globally for my work in international marketing. I use to teach her Maths. She is strongly bonded to her grandparents, cousins, and the entire extended family. We focused on her overall development. Our family friends expected her to go for technology education at IIT Bombay which is the trend in Maharashtrian middle-class families but Supriya chose commerce and management, and we supported her.

"We taught our daughter that building character is important for developing a career. We taught her value of hard work"

She is a very obedient but still rebellious child. She wants to understand the logic behind every 'family discipline' that she has to obey. But once convinced, she will implement it completely. We were so much happy to see our daughter being loved equally at her school, college, friend circle and now in the Tata group where she works. Arti and I always inspired her to do more and match her potential. We made her realize how she was a gifted child and how we choose only one child so that we can concentrate our parental efforts on her in spite of our busy corporate and academic careers. Arti and I always knew that God gifted us with world-class talent and we have to take her where she belongs. We always knew that God chose us as the parents of the corporate leader India will be proud of. Now it is a matter of her efforts, our guidance, and our family's sacrifice supported by Ganapati Bappa's blessings.

CHAPTER THREE

Leaders Don't Negotiate

People can't negotiate with leaders. They demand, request, and pursue leaders for their gains but leaders don't negotiate. Why? How do leaders push their agenda forward without negotiations? Why do they not believe in the negotiations? (This article was published on LinkedIn on 19 February 2019. Got 1831 Likes; 103 Comments; and 135 Shares)

"Leaders blend empathy with sympathy hence they tend to give more"

Philanthropists Leaders have a kind heart. Leaders constantly think about giving. Ordinary people love gifts, leaders love gifting. Leaders enjoy the happiness glittering in the eyes of receivers when they give them something. Leaders enjoy the joy of giving. They feel frustrated when they are unable to give something to someone. The source of the generosity of the leaders is their mindset. They don't have a 'mental poverty' Usually people have a 'scarcity-mind set'. They negotiate till the last penny. But leaders have an 'abundance mindset'. They feel that they have enough and they can earn enough hence they can think of giving things to others.

A secured mindset and fairness to all Trust in the God and confidence about own abilities provide leaders with an abundance mindset. This mindset provides them with a sense of security. They are at peace with themselves and also with the universe. They know there is no free lunch. They are aware of the worth of everything and have the willingness to pay for it. That is also the reason why they don't negotiate.

"Negotiating means settling for the less."

Negotiation requires either party to give up its best possible solution in favor of an optimum solution that will be acceptable to both. The process of negotiations is the process of cutting down. Leaders believe in building up rather than cutting down. They are creative and develop creative solutions to problem-solving rather than getting into negotiations for the current positions. Leaders don't settle for less. They are resourceful and always on the lookout for better solutions rather than settling with the negotiations.

"Leaders focus on win-win situations and hence are not required to negotiate"

Sensitivity Leaders are very sensitive. They have a special sensory organ that provides them with an advantage. Their sense of empathy is very high. People need not ask them. Leaders understand people and their needs, beforehand.

"Leaders focus on earning than saving. They want to earn more so that they can give more."

Leaders don't enjoy cutting, they enjoy growing Leaders don't enjoy roles where they are required to get into haggling. They delegate such work to others. Their sensitivity puts them at disadvantage in negotiations. Leader's team-mates always feel that he gets cheated by people & he is not prudent.

Commitment to Excellence They don't haggle over frugal things. Leaders don't want their people to be with them halfheartedly. They expect a hundred percent and hence provide a hundred percent. If prices are negotiated with the suppliers they would cut corners somewhere. Under-paid employees under-perform. Leaders don't accept such situations. A leader may not fulfill the greed but he can definitely satisfy the need of his people. Leaders value the human resource the most and know that the fuel for this resource is emotions. Expectations emerge out of emotions rather than physiological needs.

"Leaders are masters in 'expectations management'. For them, managing emotions is important for managing expectations"

Give two-Get four Great leaders may give double the salary but their inspiration makes people deliver the work of four people. Emotions are the bond leaders share with their team. They leverage it to manage expectations and also to avoid negotiations. People work harder because they don't want to let down their leader who shows trust in them and pays them well. A leader's trust infuses energy. When people know that their leader is dependent on them for something, they travel an extra mile and burn the midnight oil.

"Leaders have the right perception and they provide the right perspective"

IQ and Perception Leaders have a higher IQ. They have better perceptions. They can understand things much faster and much better than others. They use this advantage to educate others rather than over-powering them. They are good coaches and focus on developing the right perspectives and perceptions. Providing exposure and opportunity helps in developing a 'leader-like' perspective. After the experience, people can empathize with the leader better and stop negotiating with the leadership.

"Leaders are too strong to negotiate with"

Leaders do their homework well. They keep themselves updated. They change with time and always remain relevant. They don't let people take advantage of their lack of knowledge. If they don't understand something, they employ experts or hire consultants and learn from them. They are a unique combination of certain qualities. Leaders are the best coach but at the same time, they are the best students. People feel the scale and the muscle of leaders and give up rather than negotiate.

"Leaders inspire and make people do what they wish people to do"

Focus on inspiration rather than negotiations If the leader negotiates then people feel frustrated. For them, he is the hope. They look up to him for their aspirations. Leaders inspire people rather than negotiate with them. Leaders, open up the minds of people and make them think harder. They are the master sales persons and convince people on many difficult issues rather than negotiating with them.

"Cost cutting is painful, it generates tears, and emits negative energy. The increasing utility is delightful, it generates a smile."

Focus on increasing the utility rather than cutting costs. Businesses try to increase value in every offering. This can be done either by increasing the utility or reducing the cost or by doing both. The delivered value is the ratio of the utility to cost. Customers and other stakeholders see what utility they draw visa vice the cost they incur. The higher the ratio better is the value. Great leaders focus on increasing utility much higher than the additional cost. this provides a higher value. With suppliers, leaders deal differently. They provide higher volumes and reduce the cost per piece. They pay faster and get better deals.

"Leaders are Kangaroos. They take their people in the pouch of the tummy"

Take them all Leaders share resources and returns with everyone who helps in serving the customers. Great leaders treat employees as associates, suppliers as partners, and channel partners as members of the family. They try to maximize returns for everyone. They have happy suppliers and channel partners, delighted customers, and loyal employees. This concern for everyone puts leaders on a different pedestal. When they ask for something people can't say no to them because of the huge respect earned by them. Even very demanding leaders don't command, they request but their wish is the command for their team and associates. Leaders are hardly put into the position of negotiation.

Resourcefulness Leaders are resourceful by nature. They can find out right people, suppliers, partners, materials, etc that fit into their expectations and budgets. This resourcefulness helps them in avoiding negotiations.

CHAPTER FOUR

Leading Sung and Unsung Heroes

Organizations are built by the contributions made by the heroes and the sacrifices made by the unsung heroes. Leaders themselves are sung heroes though they would love to remain otherwise. They stand with the support of unsung heroes. How do leaders create these sung and unsung heroes? How do they create leaders? (Published on LinkedIn on 13 February 2019. Got 792 Likes; 37 Comments and 33 Shares)

"Contributions build businesses, Sacrifices build organizations"

Great businesses are built by the contributions of the team members who are associated with those businesses. Performers take businesses to great heights. Achieving scale or dominating a niche is impossible without the outstanding performances of many sung heroes. Leaders facilitate the performances by providing resources. Leaders spot performers. They smell talents. Leaders induce the talent to perform by taking out fear of the unknown. Performers are risk takers. Talent becomes a performer when takes risks. Leaders provide first-hand experiences which reduce risk perceptions. Leaders know success is a binary result of a sincere attempt. It may take values as, the success or failures. Leaders lay safety nets for top performers and provide ladders, on the safety nets, to climb back to action.

"Leaders protect the performers from personal risks."

Leaders institutionalize the risks and personalize the rewards. They groom entrepreneurship. They create a healthy atmosphere where performers feel charged and get motivated to perform. Top performances are required to take risks. Leader's safety-nets help performers jump at the impossible goals. Great leaders create an organizational culture where people stretch themselves to their limits and beyond. Leaders take out the fear of failure. They boost the morale to perform by developing a performance culture and support systems. Leaders believe that experience is a necessity for assured performances and experience is the function of exposure. They develop 'talent hunt and management programmes' for the same.

"Stretching the performance limits results in the increased potential of the person besides achieving the impossible targets"

The performers get into the game of stretching their limits and increasing their potential on a continuous basis. Such stretching exercise by many employees releases a lot of energy which is conducive to organizational growth. A leader channelizes this energy and provides direction.

"Leaders direct energies toward the mission, and cement performances to realize the vision."

Grooming entrepreneurship Great leaders nurture entrepreneurship. Such employees have a few distinct qualities which are nurtured by training, exposure, and experiences. They are charged by the mission & vision, they take ownership and risk, and they deliver stretched performances in the given time & resources. Entrepreneurship is always accompanied by autonomy. Such employees carve for autonomy.

> *"Leaders lay down policies and systems, and delegate authority and responsibilities. Ensure accountability with autonomy."*

Policies help employees to take routine decisions in line with the collective wisdom and goals. Systems ensure effective and efficient use of resources and also uniformity in the decision-making. Autonomy empowers employees with authority. Accountability ensures responsibility. Authority, responsibility, autonomy, and accountability must go hand in hand.

> *"Leaders produce leaders by sharing the mission, providing early exposure and developing the entrepreneurship"*

Great managers produce good employees but great leaders produce entrepreneurs, not just good employees. Managers produce their clones, leaders produce leaders. Employees go by policies & systems, leaders groom them to focus on business opportunities. If a must, they make exceptions with justifications. Employees seek approvals from seniors while leaders groom them to take ownership and seek concurrence. Autonomy is not absolute freedom. It provides flexibility in the decision-making to suit the context, culture, situation, business need, employee styles, etc.

> *"Performances take businesses to great heights, Sacrifices help them remain there"*

Sacrifices make great organizations Great leaders create performers and transform them into leaders. Every performer can't be the leader though. A leader has to choose a few. It is a very tough decision and requires serious trade-offs. Even the best performers can be the victims of this limited choice. Their turn may get delayed. Their recognition and rewards might miss. They have to accept other performers as emerging leaders. It can create a rift which can lead to attrition. Leaders have to handle this delicate issue carefully. But irrespective of the care taken by the leader, a few performers will be disheartened. Their reaction pattern determines the organization's fate. Some great performers digest this poison. They sacrifice their interest for organizational interests. Why could they do it when others couldn't?

"Commitment to the mission & loyalty to the leader is the foundations of sacrifice"

Organizations are built and they thrive on such valuable sacrifices of loyal performers. Sacrifices are as important as contributions. The fuel for the sacrifice is the inspiration provided by the leader. Such people have a strong sense of purpose and they don't get deviated from it, even for their personal growth. They have faith in the leader and his judgment. They are much more mature than others. They have better empathy for the leaders.

"Sung heroes contribute sweat, unsung heroes contribute blood, their personal careers for life"

Unsung heroes are emotionally hooked to the leader and to the organization. Leaders also remember such unsung heroes in the organization and always try to compensate for their sacrifice, at later date, through some other means. Unsung heroes have many 'untold' stories. Some of them become confident in the leader and remain loyal to the organization.

CHAPTER FIVE

Why are leaders fearless?

Most of us generate self-inflicting fears. These fears are usually because of unawareness rather than uncertainties. One of the most common qualities among leaders is that they are fearless. Leaders educate themselves to fight against their fears. The fearlessness makes them dare to walk firmly towards the mission. Leaders have extra energy because they conserve it rather than wasting it on fears. (Published on LinedIn on 21 January 2019. Got 461 Likes; 35 Comments and 36 Shares)

"Fear provokes a second mind and we get into the trap of a 'double mind'."

This second mind which is full of fears pulls us down and we digress from our objective. Security is mostly a mental phenomenon. There is no mechanical lock in the world that thieves can't break but we put them on our doors. I have realized that the locks are mostly for the owner of the house rather than the thief. For thieves, locks are just deterrents that delay their task.

"Most of the time fears are virtual."

Fear is the function of perception. Snake bites humans because it develops the perception of fear. Many wild animals attack humans because of their perception of threat. But perception is the function of knowledge and belief. Leaders know the sources of fear. They develop knowledge. Their beliefs are scientific, rational, and grounded in their experiences.

"Leaders know the value of everything & they also know the nuisance value of people & things they encounter."

Leaders cover their risks carefully considering the damage inflicting the power of people and other factors in the environment. They don't undermine any such factor which will challenge their plan of action. Two examples of such careful planning can be given from the life of the great Maratha worrier 'Chatrapati Shivaji Maharaj' (the Mumbai airport and the main train terminus in Mumbai are named after him). He went to meet the Mughal emperor of India (in the 17th century), Aurangzeb, in Delhi. He knew that the emperor wasn't trustworthy and would play a foul in spite of the promise given to him by the Rajput king about the safety and security of his life, on behalf of the king. When Shivaji Maharaj walked off from the meeting due to insult inflicted on him by the poor protocol, the emperor put him in jail in Agra. But Shivaji Maharaj couldn't be detained beyond a few days. He absconded with his son, Sambhaji, using an unimaginable trick that was carefully planned as a crisis plan. (Read more about it on the internet or in Indian history books).

"Great leaders fight fears with careful planning and meticulous execution"

A powerful warrior of the Mughal king from Bijapur (Karnataka), Afzal Khan ruined many Hindu temples and inflicted atrocities on the citizens of the Maratha kingdom. He challenged Shivaji Maharaj. The fearless Maratha King agreed to meet him personally. Shivaji Maharaj knew Afzal Khan well. He wasn't surprised when Afzal Khan suddenly attacked him with a knife, during the meeting, in which nobody was expected to carry weapons. Shivaji Maharaj was ready for the incident and counter-attacked Afzal only to kill him in a few minutes. Shivaji Maharaj was a great leader who always knew the nuisance power of his enemies & never underestimated their lack of trustworthiness in spite of tall promises given to him.

"Threats trigger excitement among leaders rather than fear. They demonstrate mettle through their fearless actions."

Leaders are very excited about the opportunities in the environment. Such possibilities excite them so much that they don't feel threatened by the threats posed by the environment. 'Sense of security' is the second most important human need after physiological needs. We want to secure everything we have. We fear losing them or somebody snatching them from us. The billions of dollars of insurance businesses thrive on our sense of insecurity.

"'The fear of the unknown' is our main enemy. It forces us to waste our resources on creating a 'false sense of security'"

Leaders overcome their fears They know their mission can't be realized unless they have God's blessings. Once they get it they become fearless. Shivaji Maharaj always said that the Hindu sovereign state was the wish of God & his mission was to fulfill the wish of God. He was never defeated in his life by any warrior in a one-to-one encounter on the battlefield. Hindus believe that it was because of his bravery and also due to the sword given to him by the goddess Durga (Bhavani Mata). She wanted him to eliminate the enemies who troubled people & inflicted atrocities on them. Shivaji Maharaj's mission for the Hindu empire was the blessings of God. He fought fearlessly because he was fighting for the cause given to him by God. He aligned his mission with the wish of God and became fearless.

Commitment to conviction. Great leaders have great conviction. They commit themselves to their conviction. They tune themselves with the ultimate truth and chase it fearlessly.

"Leaders value what is right for their people rather than what is liked by them. It requires following the conviction fearlessly."

Visionary corporate leaders believed in delivering what is good for their customers rather than what is demanded by them. They said customers know their problems better but are not aware of the perfect solution. The companies have to provide the right solution. But this conviction required fearless self-belief. They dared to swim upstream, against the current, fearlessly to become the legends who went into the history books. Chinese believed 'online' will not work in China until Jack Ma made Alibaba one of the largest online players in the world. Apple's choice of a different operating system could be proved suicidal until Steve Jobs made it a grand success. Leaders are comfortable with uncertainties They know the theory of relativity well and how things work. They believe security is relative, uncertainty is constant. Leaders develop the power to progress under uncertainty. They enjoy the challenge posed by uncertainty. They look at the changing market situations as opportunities. They are at peace with themselves. Leaders know who they are, what can they do, and what they can't do. They also have great patience to wait for their turn. They are never in a hurry though hate procrastination. Leaders believe in organic growth. But they don't hesitate for inorganic growth, whenever it is a must.

"The leaders empower people, develop and trust the team"

Great leaders create great teams. Both leaders and their teams install a sense of security in each other. Leaders create other leaders who have the competencies to take the mission further. Such leaders provide the required contribution and sacrifice. Great leaders have no fear of failure because of such leaders. Shivaji Maharaj created leaders like Baji Prabhu Deshpande, Tanaji Malusare, Yesaji Kank, and many more. Sam Walton created a strong team and many leaders. When he passed away Walmart's turnover was $50 Billion in the early 1990s, today it has grown more than 10 times in less than 20 years. Sam's team and leaders created by him contributed to this growth. The leader provides a strong policy that helps his team to make day-to-day decisions. He delegates functions and powers to his team and establishes proper systems and processes which respond to the dynamic changes. Great leaders are great planners. They factor in all eventualities and become fearless.

CHAPTER SIX

Leaders: At Peace with Themselves

The leaders are always at peace with themselves. They know what they can do and what they can't. Leaders clearly know their mission, their path, the resources they need, and also how to get those resources. Leaders are not just obsessed with the mission but they also cherish their journey towards the mission. Leaders have the capability to understand the milestones in the journey. Those milestones ensure that they are on the right path. They know very well when to accelerate and also how to slow down. (Published on LinkedIn on 29 November 2018. Got 518 Likes; 24 Comments and 33 Shares)

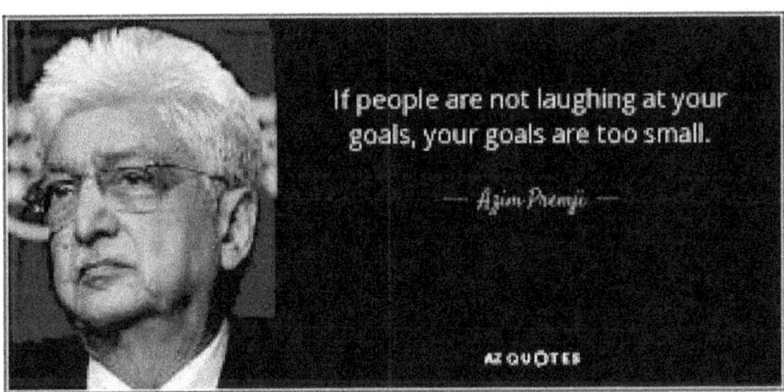

These captains calmly put on the 'seat belt sign when they hit turbulence and others get shaken up by the jerks from the rough weather. What is the source of their calmness? Few things come to leaders as their own in-born qualities & the rest, they acquire in their journey of leadership. Leaders draw their energy from their mission & vision. Faith in the vision & mission keeps them at peace. They seek God's blessing through the nobility of intentions and eagerness to make difference in people's life. A leader is at peace because he makes his mission a spiritual journey. Vision becomes reality only when it gets God's blessings. The leader has to do the rest through his team. Realization of these facts gives the leader peace of mind. Leaders are at peace with themselves because they connect & understand their mission spiritually. They delegate a major part of their task to God and get peace of mind. No wonder Lord Tirupati Balaji is the business partner in many of the south Indian companies. About 15 to 16 years ago my friend and I worked as professors in the same B school. We had a carpool. We used to drive together, every day for 3 hours, to and fro. Thanks to Mumbai traffic and the Vikroli-Jogeshwari Link Road construction. After just a few months he left the job and went back to a full-time corporate career. In a few years, he became CEO and then a Managing Director of a German company operating in India. I am always proud of his achievements. Recently, I asked him two questions, his response made me think and write this article.

"How is the world different for him after becoming head of the organization? "

"What is the most difficult task he is facing as the leader?"

I am writing about the first question in this article. For the second question I will write a separate article, 'What is a leader's job?' How is the world different for leaders? Professionals set their minds on becoming leaders. From day one of their careers, they aspire and work for getting into the leadership saddle. They look at the organizational mission and vision as the derived objective that they would need to handle after becoming the leader. It is impossible to visualize how would the earth look from the moon unless we land up on the moon. From the earth, the sky looks blue and the moon looks white, from the moon earth looks blue and the sky looks dark black. A leader's perspective is like the view from the moon. It is radically different than his employees who have earth's view. Professional employees just can't think of the leader's perspective. Companies have been hammering hard to develop entrepreneurship DNA and approach among their employees but it is a far cry even for the best of the best organizations. Employees always think their growth and organizational mission are two different things. They focus on their JDs and KRAs missing the total picture. They fail to understand the leader's view that the sum of parts is not equal to the whole.

"Only leaders realize, that their growth is directly related to the organizational mission."

My consultancy experience tells me that the employees of the small and medium scale organization have a better entrepreneurship approach. That may be the reason why aspirants of entrepreneurship prefer to work with SMEs. The professionals keep thinking about their careers, juggling their packages, and struggle with their tax planning. Once they hit the leadership board slowly they start realizing the futility of these things. The major transformation of the employees takes place when they hit the leadership pole. The thinking transforms from 'career orientation' to 'mission orientation'.

"The corporate journey remains on the career path only till the leadership milestone."

The transformed employees start thinking about 'us' rather than about 'me'. They are worried about organizational mission and vision rather than their own career, package, and taxes. Abraham Maslow nicely captured this in his theory of hierarchy of the human needs. He suggested that the ultimate need of any human is the spiritual 'self-actualization' need which comes after fulfilling the materialistic 'esteem need'.

"The leadership journey becomes a spiritual journey. In the end, a business leader gets transformed into a corporate saint"

Mahatma Gandhi fulfilled his esteem need after going to England and completing the highest degree in law. He was a successful lawyer in South Africa when he was thrown out of the train and climbed Maslow's hierarchy of human needs to get charged by self-esteem. Coming back to India, the leadership transformed him from 'Barrister Gandhi' to 'Mahatma Gandhi'. he was transformed from a three-piece suit to khadi Pancha. Leadership made him spiritual. He started singing prayers every morning and committed himself to humanity. A similar transformation happened to Mother Teresa and Dalai Lama. These social and religious leaders became saints.

> *"Great leaders realize that corporate social responsibility (CSR) isn't enough. Personnel social responsibility is also required."*

Why do great corporate leaders get into charity?

Even the business leaders who try hard to earn every single penny realize that money is a tool and not the mission. They get into charity in a big way. The Indian business tycoon and leader of the software giant, Wipro, Azim Premji donated tens of thousands of crores to charity going way ahead of the 'zakat' suggested by his religion. By donating Rs 27,514/- crore to become the most generous Indian by giving away half of his wealth for the cause of education in India. Tata Sons, the holding company of Tatas spend more than two third of their profits on charity, every year and which they have been doing for many decades. Thanks to the legacy of J R D Tata, the all-time great business leader of India.

> *"The leadership journey makes them understand, that humanity has more power than money."*

Why leaders are at peace with themselves Once the business leaders are transformed into corporate saints they develop immense internal strength. They start getting peace from within. They often experience the power of God. They know that they are the tool and not the artisan. They develop many 'sub-conscious competencies' which are unique and also help their businesses in a big way. They can smell the business environment well. Due to their stature, they can manage regulators well. They can identify talent fast. They groom future leaders carefully. Investors trust them with any amount of money. Great leaders raise resources much faster than others. When Dhirubhai Ambani dreamt to start the largest refinery at Jamnagar, Reliance was required to raise Rs 25,000/- cr. It appeared very difficult task but was made easy by Dhirubhai. He promised and raised that money from the market. The Reliance share was oversubscribed in the primary market. Dhirubhai became the God of investors, employees, suppliers, and dealers. He never cheated them. In fact, many of them became millionaires while Dhirubhai became a Billionaire.

"Leaders are spiritual, if not religious. They know how the universe is governed by its leader and also the underlying principles."

This knowledge makes them at peace. They know what can work and what can't. They also know that they can't control the outcome completely. There is strong frictional force and inertia which are required to overcome. Great leaders know that they can't be always lucky & they will have their share of failures. But their strong survival instinct overpowers failures. Leaders survive for their mission. It is the purpose of the existence of the organization and also of the leader.

"Great leaders maintain nobility of intention. It makes the luck flip in their favor"

Nobel missions get the support of God's wish. It induces the power in the mission and leaders draw this power from their mission. Business leaders are Wealth creators. They also distribute wealth and change the lives of hundreds and thousands of people. Their vision relates to people, making their life better, wealthier, and happier. Vision is the virtual picture. A picture in the future. Only the leaders see it in present hence they know it is not impossible. Leaders never doubt vision. It is their third eye.

"The mission is a purpose, vision is the dream."

The mission is a leader's bridge to vision. They want to make the virtual vision a reality, hence they get strongly committed to the mission. Vision looks like a dream, mission looks impossible. Most of people feel both vision & mission are abstract, unreal, and impossible. But they are leaders' faith. Vision & mission make the leader spiritual. They connect the leader to God. They are his intentions. He gets blessings because of the purity of his intentions. They are the tools that give power to the leader & people follow them. Vision and mission never work unless they get God's blessings. Once it is done, leaders do the rest through their team. The great leaders are aware of these connections hence they are at peace, It is the foundation of their confidence.

> *"The mission rests on the willpower of the leaders. Hope is the fuel that drives it."*

Leaders are faithful to their mission. That is the reason the leaders are 'never-give-up' types. They expect to meet rough weather and are always prepared for it. When the wind blows against them, the leader's focus is on minimum loss and damage control. It is part of their life hence leaders are at peace with themselves. Faith is the source of the leader's calmness. Leaders know that the rough sea makes great sailors. Leaders know that they are just the first runners in the relay race. They will have to pass on the baton to another team player.

> *"Leaders build their teams, hold on to them in slowdowns and fight odds with the core competencies of the team."*

Leaders are masters of delegation. Micro-management is not for the leaders. They understand the difference between 'meticulous execution' & micro-management. They have unique skills to do meticulous execution through delegation.

In Short, Leaders are at peace with themselves because they make their journey towards the mission, a spiritual experience. They seek God's blessings. Do meticulous execution without getting into micro-management. They draw their power from the mission and vision, They seek God's blessings by the nobility of their intentions. They partner with God and know what they can do and what God will do. They also know what the team has to do and what the team will do. Their ability to develop a strong team and a strong faith keep them at peace with themselves. Their perspective is unique. They add value through their perspective and life experiences. Hence they are irreplaceable and secure. That security adds to their peace.

CHAPTER SEVEN

Silence: A Leader's Wisdom

Great leaders use words like money and transactions like ATM machines, and the environment with only bare minimum words. They want people to tell them problems in the way the leader wants to listen. long stories are not welcomed by them. Many people go to a leader with the same problems hence he is usually aware of the background and the issue. That is the reason why the leader wants people to skip an introduction and come straight to the point. As a professional grows in the organization and moves up the ladder he realizes, 'Less is more. For him, words are an important resource. He hardly or sparingly uses it. How do they do it? (Published on LinkedIn on 6 November 2018. Got 252 Likes; 25 Comments 44 Shares)

Creative writers express themselves in beautiful words. Poets express much more in much lesser words. Philosophers say everything is just a 'one-liner'. As a person moves up on the intelligence/ talent scale, he realizes inadequacy of words, limitations of diction, and constraints of articulation. He realizes everything of this is subjected to misinterpretation. Secondly, he hates cliche and wants to optimize his time, he wants to get into action rather than just discussing problems. He wants to attend to more people and listen to more problems. He develops a skill to communicate differently, with minimum words or preferably with no words at all. Great leaders use words like money and transactions like ATM machines, and the environment with only bare minimum words. They want people to tell them problems in the way the leader wants to listen. long stories are not welcomed by them. Many people go to a leader with the same problems hence he is usually aware of the background and the issue. That is the reason why the leader wants people to skip an introduction and come straight to the point. As a professional grow in the organization and moves up the ladder he realizes, 'Less is more'. For him, words are an important resource. He hardly or sparingly uses it. How do they do it? they will try to leverage the situation, or mood prevailing in the environment or they will use some non-verbal communication instead. Artists are masters in non-verbal communication. A photographer uses just a lens, and a few strokes of a brush to express the feelings of a painter. I am always amazed by the silent precision in the operation theatre in the hospital. Doctors and nurses develop non-verbal skills with great empathy and teamwork.

> **"Leaders communicate through eyes, facial expressions, body language, touch, or even through the silence"**

One of my uncles worked as a very senior politician, holding a critical cabinet minister position in the Govt. of India. He also was the head of the Maharashtra state as a Chief Minister. I observed him carefully, since childhood, he could remember short messages better and tended to forget verbose articulations. His senior Dr. Manmohan Singh, the prime minister of India was also the same.

> **"Leaders are obsessed with giving, it is their strong need. They are sharp & sense the needs of people who go to them."**

The trick to remaining in their memory is to speak less and use a few words. In conversations leaders would hardly speak, they focus on listening and identifying your needs. People will have to do more homework when the boss speaks less. Speaking less requires more preparation than speaking at a length. Even experienced speakers practice well when they go live on TV or radio shows.

"Silence is a state when the mind and body stop dispensing energy. They start gathering and consolidating the cosmic energy"

Why do leaders love silence? Leaders are mostly with people. Silence is the time when they can be with themselves. They can talk to themselves in silence. They can reflect on many aspects. Silence provides a conducive environment for creative thinking.

Silence is not emptiness. There is a difference between being dumb and being silent. Dumb people are compelled to keep mum. They don't speak because they know that they are hollow, they don't have the required substance. But a silent person remains so by his choice. Silence is not about the emptiness. A man who is silent in spite of being full is a man of wisdom. There is a strong reason behind his silence. His facial expressions and body language will reflect his wisdom. He maintains his wisdom soaked in silence. His wisdom gets reflected in his eyes.

"A man with wisdom takes control through his eyes. He doesn't need rosy words"

Sleeping is remaining inactive. Silence is remaining active but in a mute Sleeping is resting, both, mind and body. It is necessary for the recovery of the lost energy. It is a pause that is necessary for life. Sleep is mandatory, silence is voluntary. Silence is stopping the physical stimulus. But it doesn't mean remaining dull. A silent person is an active person. Silence only means stopping the inward-out communication and facilitating outward-in communication. It means changing the focus from self to others and caring about what others want to tell you rather than what you want to tell others. Being silent means changing your mode from delivery to receipt.

Silence-A Leadership Wisdom: Great leaders can read the language of silence very well. They know what is obvious is not apparent because of the silence of some critical persons. Great leaders know why some team members don't speak. Great leaders know that those who don't speak are likely to know more. May be because such people are at a higher intellectual level. Others can't see what they can see because others are vertically challenged. They don't speak because they look at the total picture. They wonder whether people who are looking at parts would appreciate the total picture. The third possibility is that those who speak less have better perception hence they tend to understand things quite differently than others. But such people are always in minority. They are outnumbered by others. How people debate depends on their personality and taste. Shallow people get into a fierce fight to prove their point. They project their low-confidence as high-confidence. They resort to teaming up to create a majority. They use other tools like strong words, abusive language, high tone & volume. They always attempt to personalize the arguments rather than restrict them to the issue. People with wisdom don't replicate this strategy. They prefer not to waste their time on such people. Some people believe their speech shall not make any difference and its effectiveness shall not have any bearing on the outcome. This can happen due to the culture of the organization or leadership style or polarisation of views or due to some vested interest that governs the outcome of the decision. Smart people realize when the speech is silver but the silence is golden.

> *"Silence requires closing the mouth and opening the mind."*

A leader can be silent but not calm. Being silent means not expressing views verbally, being calm means managing emotions & not showing emotions. Silence breeds calmness which helps in managing emotions. Leaders are masters in emotion management. Silence helps them in emotion management strategy.

Cross Talking- Leaders irritant Leaders maintain silence when you speak & they expect the same when they speak. They hate when people talk among themselves when the leader speaks.

> *"Cross-talking is like driving a car in the no-entry, against the traffic, in the same lane."*

In a nutshell, while dealing with the leaders don't unnecessarily intrude into their silence zone. Help them in maintaining silence, it is their source of energy. When a leader speaks listen carefully. Don't cross-talk with anybody while the leader speaks. You should speak only when your turn comes. Try to use fewer words. Stick to the point, say what is the issue & what you want. Don't waste time giving background and repeating the same points again. Leaders remember short messages hence be as short as possible. In a professional meeting identify a quiet person, and encourage him to speak. There is a chance that he has better knowledge or valuable perspective. People keep quiet for their reasons. Great leaders identify such people and motivate them to speak. They might come out with great points.

Teaching Leaders Their Business

I started teaching MBA students ever since my daughter, Supriya, was in school. She used to wonder, whom did I teach? What did I teach? Probably those were the most difficult question posed to a management professor. I ask myself do I teach Marketing? or Retailing or Sales? Why do I go to my class? What is one thing that I do in my class? Over a period of time, when she grew up, I developed an answer. (Published on LinkedIn on 23 July 2017. Got 1,654 Likes; 52 Comments and 261 Shares)

"Teaching management is teaching business. Teaching management is producing leaders. Teaching management is teaching leaders their business."

Teaching various management subjects is important but teaching business is more important. Most of the management teachers can't see the forest for the trees. They are too much worried about their subject and miss the purpose of their students behind attending the class. Students want to know how they use your inputs in business. How can you develop ease of doing business by imparting the domain knowledge? There is a difference between teaching science and teaching management or commerce.

"Science students are passionate about knowledge. Business students want to use knowledge to create wealth."

Science is a systematic body of knowledge. It has a chain of information. Many chains get connected to each other and create a structure of knowledge. Science teachers walk their students through this structure of knowledge. Science students are obsessed with 'why'. Management students want to know 'how'. They can stay with not knowing 'why' as long as they know 'how'.

"In science, things work as per theory. In management what works becomes a theory"

Management students visualize their education differently. They expect their teachers to share what works in the business. They want to connect the classroom to the marketplace. They want to extend the classroom to a share market.

"Management students want their classroom to be transformed into a boardroom."

They want the classroom discussions like boardroom discussions. They want to think like businessmen. They don't want to climb each branch of the tree of knowledge. Their ecstasy is trekking through the forest for the treasure hunt. Their treasure is wealth, their treasure is business development. Their treasure is their career as an entrepreneur or successful business executives. Students of the current generation are very objective. They want to move towards their treasure every day, in every class.

"Students listen to you only if you give them a clue about their treasure hunt."

A few teachers complain about poor student attention in business school classrooms. Students expect teachers to understand their priority and not impose an academic priority upon them. An Indian professor friend was debating with me on the job of a management teacher. He believes our job is getting into a class and teaching. Why does the university expect academicians to do research, publish papers, conduct management development programs, and get into consulting? Probably he has not thought about his job. Are we a teaching shop? Are we teaching the textbook?

"Students want you to share the insight and not just a textbook theory."

They can read American business management books but they want to know what will work in India. How do we adapt the global management knowledge to the Indian business situations? Today students are resourceful. they have google, they have YouTube, and they have Wikipedia. Can you take them beyond Google? This needs research. This needs consulting. Research and consulting can help in developing business insights. The research will keep teachers up to date. Consulting can help them know what can work in real-life business and what can't. During the conference presentations, you can validate your insights. Management Development Programmes can be a tool to impress industry leaders and develop networking. These are different ways to develop insights. A good teacher develops business insights using these tools and technics

"Great teachers produce great business leaders by providing a strong foundation of business insights."

Insights develop wisdom. Teachers share management wisdom and help their students make decisions. They develop the right perceptions. These perceptions develop a business perspective. The perspective is important in decision-making.

Teaching Leaders the Art of Decision Making The leaders can be trained in the art of decision-making by developing the right perceptions and perspectives. They help in deciding what is right and what is wrong. They also guide in fixing the wrong. Decision-making is choosing from the available options. Many times the alternatives are not very clear and well defined. Some alternatives are obvious but not apparent. Business leaders are required to develop alternatives. They have to be taught that every alternative has a flip side, it comes with side effects too. The subject knowledge can be very useful here.

> *"Great business management teachers teach their students how to use the domain/subject knowledge in wealth creation."*

Management teachers train their students to pluck the roses and leave the thrones. Pick the opportunity and kick the threat. It requires a strong foundation of domain knowledge. Great teachers teach decision-making through structured domain knowledge. They teach how to make the subject knowledge work in real-life business situations. They teach that no alternative is either 'good' or 'bad'. Alternatives are not opposites. It is overly risky to ignore some options completely to choose another alternative.

> *"Everybody may have a different decision-making parameter because his or her situations are different."*

Even if two people have the same situation their decisions are different because their perceptions are different, their values are different or their cultures are different. As a result, their decision-making parameters are different. There are variables in the environment. They are required to be forecasted. Their future values are required to be estimated. They determine the framework for decision-making. These things are required to be taught in the business management class. That can happen only if the teachers develop scholarships, conduct research, attend conferences, and write and get their publications reviewed by peers. The most important thing is that the teacher has to take these things to the classroom. The delivery of the teacher should rise above PowerPoint presentations.

> *"Great teachers develop power in their points while others are developing PowerPoint presentations."*

Students love such a 'power pack professor' rather than the 'slide show professor' who is just a teaching shop.

CHAPTER NINE

Leader – Changing Potential Energy to Kinetic

In my last article on leadership, 'Too many Kings Can Ruin The Army', (Printed in Part-1) I wrote about how leaders and managers are different, how they complement each other, and how leadership is the next 'avatar' of a manager's evolution process. I just touched upon the differences between 'professionals' and 'entrepreneurs'. In this article, I want to discuss what are those rare leadership qualities. What makes the leader outstanding, rather standout? (Published on LinkedIn on 15 Oct 2015. Got 126 Likes; 19 Comments and 64 Shares)

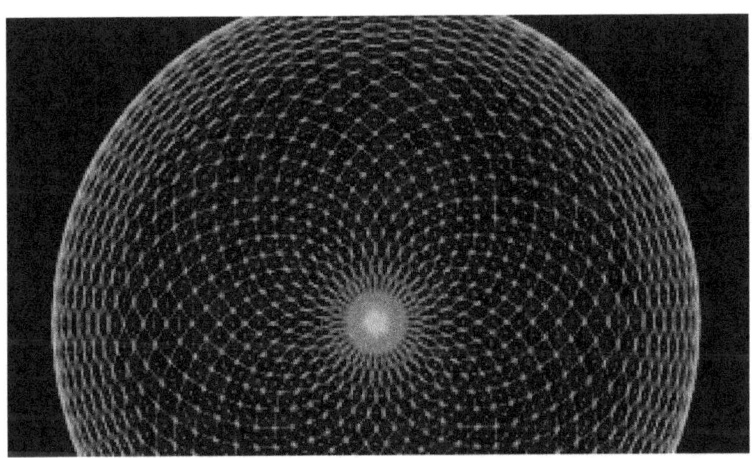

Leader: Changing Potential Energy to Kinetic Energy: The law of science says, 'Energy can be neither created nor be destroyed, but it transforms from one form to another'. For instance chemical energy can be converted to kinetic energy in the explosion of a stick of dynamite. Leader applies this law to human beings. The leader identifies people with potential energy, sets them in action and creates a situation wherein their potential energy changes into kinetic energy. People with potential (energy) have inertia. Another law of Physics says, 'unless acted upon by some external force, body maintains its state of inertia.' A leader is that force which helps in getting rid of inertia. He sets a body in action.

Leaders are at peace with themselves: I am yet to meet a confused leader. They know who they are and who they are not. They also know what they can do, what they cannot. They have reasons for their actions and inactions. They know what to expect from themselves. This makes leaders look very calm and composed. They know what they are doing and why they are doing it. They know, they are just pawns and real power comes from the God. They are internally excited but like the deep ocean.

Most of the leaders are spiritual. They experience Almighty's power. They are the chosen ones. But they do not know why. They know, they will arrive but do not know when. They know they will do it but do not know how. They know some day they are going to make it big but do not know how big. They are 'corporate monks'.

Man on Mission: Leaders swear by their mission. It is the purpose of their life. They will give up anything and everything for their mission. They never age, neither physically nor mentally. Their team always wonders about their source of energy. They draw power from their mission. Many leaders disappeared after their mission was accomplished. It happened to Mahatma Gandhi, Churchill and to many others. Where is Gorbachev today?

Man Who Saw Tomorrow: Leaders live their dreams. They see what others cannot. They can see how the world will look like when the mission is accomplished. They, probably, have some organ which we do not have. Hence we can't see what they can.

First Comes the Team then the Family: The leader knows that when he is thrown to the wall his team comes to the rescue. He always belongs to the team. Many a times he trades-off family life and priorities for the team and for the mission. The ownership is inherited, leadership is not. The real treasure, ' The Wisdom of Leadership', stays with his team, it hardly goes to his family. That is why his successor is groomed in the team and is rarely brought up in the family.

Dealer in Hope: For the team, leader embodies hope. Napoleon Bonaparte said, "A leader is a dealer in hope". Leaders never give up. They are the first to step on the battlefield and last to step off. They are the insulators, providing constant protection to the team. They are optimists. They will tell you, "Go the extra mile, it's never crowded." We have always seen Michael Jordan, Kobe Bryant and Lebron James scoring the winning basket, for the trailing team in the last couple of seconds. Everybody gives up but they don't. Installing the sense of purpose is their way to provide hope. Leaders show possibilities. Leaders are jack of many things. They know how to make things work. They know the circumstances specific to their organization. They know what can work for their organisation and what cannot.

Can Stay with the Problem: Leaders know that they cannot solve all problems. They develop an ability to stay with problems. They know that sometimes solving a problem can generate many others. Hence it is better to stay with them. US invaded Afghanistan and Iraq to solve problems but they could only change the nature of the problem. Having learnt this lesson, the hard way, they are, now, not attempting to solve the problems in North Korea and Syria.

Better Emotion Management: Leaders are very emotional. That may be the reason why they can understand their people well. But their emotion management skills are extraordinary. They laugh out loud but cry in private. They know the prize of smile, the cost of anger and the value of tears. They know when and what to commit and omit. They observe restraint. Their reaction pattern is different. They do not jump to react immediately. They speak less, listen more. Hence whenever they speak everybody listens carefully. Many leaders are not great orators but still people love to listen to them because they speak from their heart.

Good Teacher, Good Student: Leaders have very good learning ability. They learn quickly. They accept their lack of knowledge candidly and seek assistance of specialists. But they pose intelligent questions to specialists and make them think harder. Leaders are good teachers. They know who the slow learners in their organization are. They provide required support to such employees, spend time with them to the extent that other employees feel that the leader is biased. But the leaders know that the speed of the navy is determined by the lowest ship. Leaders provide challenging opportunities and exposure to performers. Whenever they interact with their team on certain issues, they provide a different perspective. They are respected for their value additions. Only the leadership position can bring this advantage to problem solving. Leaders dance with their team but always a step ahead.

He sees a holiday in his job: He knows that he is the torchbearer and cannot relax. Henry Ford said, "Give me a man who sings on his job." Leader is such a person. For him, every day is a working day, every day is a holiday. Those who do not share his dreams find it very difficult to work closely with him. Only a few adjust to the leader's work-style, work-load and can empathize with him. Such members of the team stay longer and become leader's preferences. They form 'informal organization' or 'inner circle' and take control, irrespective of their formal designations. Some also exploit this situation for personal benefit, become powerful but finally get what they deserve. It happened to Mao, Hitler and to many other corporate leaders too. Change in the leadership also results in change in the organization structure, for this reason.

Having identified so many qualities of leaders, we must understand that leaders are not clones. They have different styles. Leaders' approach also changes in different cultures. Mao's leadership style could not have worked in American freedom struggle. Stalin's style of leadership would fail in India. Leaders belong to people. Hence their leadership styles emerges from the local culture. Chinese people have accepted 'capitalistic communism' style leaders. They do not feel suffocated. Cubans were happy with Fidel Castro. Leadership changes with culture, time, geography.

CHAPTER TEN

Why do 'Men on Mission' deliver?

We identify a few people as crazy people. Their craze is the mission they chase. Crazy people write history. Why do these crazy people deliver the result? Why do they achieve what others don't? What is the source of their energy? What are their tools? What are their methods? They are the men on a mission. **(The term is used for both genders)** (Published on LinkedIn on 26 November 2017. Got 1,401 Likes; and 102 Comments; 204 Shares)

We see a lot of people with clear goals in their life. They are clear about their objective and try to pursue that goal sincerely. But they fail in spite of having the required resources and a team, in repeated attempts. Some people succeed in their goals in spite of all the odds, with little resources, and sometimes against giant competitors. Why?

"A goal is the desired result. A mission is the purpose of existence."

Goals are desires, the mission is a compulsion. Some people are men on a mission. They scale up their goals; they convert their goal into their mission. The difference lies in the level of commitment and the gravity of the expectation.

"When a desire develops into a self-imposed compulsion, a goal becomes the mission"

A mission is stronger than goals. It is more intense. Liking develops goals but a mission is driven by passion. By definition, passion is a strong and uncontrollable emotion. The DNA of passion makes the mission so strong and uncontrollable. Goals can be reviewed, revisited, modified, revised, or radically changed. The mission can't be changed. The mission is very stiff and stubborn.

"A goal is an orientation, the mission is an attitude, deeply rooted."

A goal is a smolder, a mission is a fire hence it is wild. Goals can let you take a rest, mission always keeps you awake. Once you set goals you feel relieved because goals are specific, measurable, and achievable in a certain span of time. They are time bound. A mission can only be achieved by breaking it into a set of goals. By doing this you can pacify the fire.

"Goals can be transit stopovers, the mission is the final destination."

A goal generates another goal because it is time-bound. Mission has no expiry. It takes longer to achieve the mission. In the case of goals, you can show the progress and justify the optimum level of achievement.

> *"Managers set goals, leaders set mission."*

Goals are operational hence managers set them. The mission is strategic, hence leaders deal with them. Goals form a chain. The mission is a hook. The existence of the organization is hooked to the mission. When you achieve any goal it becomes a hygiene factor. It doesn't excite you further. You look for another goal. Thus goals always come in a bunch. The mission is always single. It excites you for life. It is a strong hook and a person gets clung to it. It always remains fresh and keeps the person fresh.

> *"The mission is always binary. It can take only two values, 'accomplished' or 'failed'."*

The leaders are identified with their mission. They virtually die when their mission gets accomplished. Do you know whether Niel Armstrong is still alive? We know, he was the first man who walked on the moon.What happened to him after he accomplished the mission? We don't know.

> *"The mission is the goal at the gunpoint."*

The mission takes sweat & blood. Goals are set by brains. A mission is set by the heart. Goal shows eagerness, mission shows desperation. Goals need a strong contribution in terms of systematic and consistent efforts with the required resources. A mission also needs it but it goes beyond.

> *"A mission needs contribution and sacrifice."*

The terrorist-like attitude Men on a mission have terrorist-like attitudes. For them their mission is everything. They don't really care for the leadership position and the authority. They take up the responsibility themselves and trade off the authority for the accomplishment of their mission.

> *"For the men on mission, the mission is larger than the leadership."*

Neither Bill Gates nor Warren Buffet is CEO of the organization. They have delegated the authority to competent leaders but retained the ownership of their mission.

> *"For men on mission, the mission is sacrosanct. They don't let even their self-interest interfere with their mission."*

Goals need sweat to achieve them, a mission also needs sweat but it can't be accomplished unless people sacrifice. Men on mission sacrifice many things to achieve their mission.

> *"Goals are difficult but a mission is near impossible."*

The mission is the purpose of life. For the men on a mission, their mission is their life. It is their identity. They are born for it, live for it and they get out of public life once they accomplish their mission.

Mission provides the energy For the men on a mission, their mission provides them the energy. They draw their energy from their mission.

> *"Leaders use the mission as a convex lens. They generate energies through mission"*

A science lesson which we did in our schools. When we hold a convex lens, at a specific distance from the paper, the rays emitting from the sun would converge to a specific point on the paper and within a few seconds, the paper starts burning.

The leaders know that their mission is like a convex lens. It concentrates the resources on the task and the task gets accomplished. The stronger lens produces fire faster. A stronger mission is required for achieving the desired result. Leaders know very well that only concentrated efforts would produce the results.

> *"Mission catches cosmic energy and focuses it on the target to produce the result."*

like the lens catches the solar energy & focuses it to produce fire. The men on mission know very well that they need not waste time worrying about the resources. The resources follow. Resources are like solar energy, they are in abundance but scattered and required to be focused using the lens called to mission.

The man who saw tomorrow A man on a mission is 'a man who saw tomorrow'. They can clearly see what others can't. In management cliche, it is called 'Vision'. Our management professors refer to such leader as a 'visionary'. They can see how the world would look like after their mission gets realized.

The tools of men on a mission They only have two lenses, convex, and conclave. They do magic with this tool. They create fire with a convex lens and see tomorrow by placing convex and conclave lenses together. Galileo Galilee made the first refracting telescope for space study, in 1609. He discovered the four largest of the moons orbiting Jupiter. Galileo also used his refracting telescope to map mountains and craters on the surface of the moon, confirmed the phases of Venus, observed and analyzed sunspots, and discovered that the Milky Way, thought at that time to be nebulous, was actually a multitude of stars packed so densely that they appeared to be clouds to the naked eye. Galileo could see objects 20 times smaller than the human eye could, using a telescope. Galileo was a man on a mission. (Credits: http://www.fortworthastro.com/beginner5.html). He saw tomorrow. He was hanged to death for rejecting the claim that the Earth is flat. He was the first human to see the round earth.

Method of the men on a mission They create & lead energies. That is their method. They inspire people by giving them a mission. They charge people using cosmic energy. People follow the men on a mission and provide them the energy.

Moral of the story. Men on mission deliver because they have a strong commitment to their mission. They live and die for their mission. They worship their mission. If they have to choose between the leadership and the mission they choose their mission. Such a strong sense of commitment develops terrorist-like attitudes within them. They become fearless, they develop desperation. Men on mission know that the mission is binary. It can only succeed or fail, there is no midway. Hence they leave no stone unturned. Their tool is two lenses, convex and concave. With a convex lens, they gather resources and focus them on their mission. With a concave lens, they see what others can't. They become visionary and see the future, wherein their mission becomes a reality. Men on mission are not really worried about the resources. Their real resource is cosmic energy. They know other resources follow. Their method is simple. They create and lead energies. People give them energies which is the real resource of the men on a mission.

Leadership Style: Online or Offline

Is leading from the front the only best strategy? To what extent the physical presence of the leader matter? Is it a must? Can the leader lead from the war room or a boardroom? I call leading from the front as 'Online leadership' and leading from the boardroom or the war room as 'leading in Absentia' or 'Offline Leadership'. (Published on LinkedIn on 8 January 2018. Got 436 Likes; 51 Comments and 82 Shares)

Online Leadership: Leading From the Front.

The physical presence of the leader spreads the aroma of his personality. His followers recognize his presence through this aroma. Soldiers are emotional folks. They feel the support of the leader when he is with them on the field. A similar feeling is shared by junior employees of the organizations who have lesser conceptual skills. They feel safe and charged when they see their leader alongside when they are working hard in the field.

> *"The field marshal draws his power from his soldiers who win many battles and push the team towards victory in the war."*

Usually the approach of 'leading from the front' works with the team which is high on emotions. Their fuel is emotions. The leader has to constantly keep them 'full tank' on emotions. Their emotional outburst keeps them going. If not controlled properly they can be 'unguided missiles' and create damage on either side.

> *"Emotional people are difficult to control from a remote location."*

Field marshals have the power to ignite emotions and also to channelize emotions towards the organizational goals. They are hands-on leaders. See here the best war field leader, in Indian history, in the photograph. Prime Minister Indira Gandhi with Field Marshal Sam Manekshaw.

> *"Field leaders have a gift of gab. They memorize the team by their rhetoric."*

Field leaders also have power in their touch. They touch the sentiments of their followers by shaking hands or by hugging. They boss around by putting their hand on the shoulders of their team members. The field leaders prepare their strategy on the field. They have an advantage. They know the situation well. They know what can work better. They can conserve the time which could be wasted while working on unworkable options.

"Field leaders hit the nail exactly on the head because they have first-hand information which is not filtered and altered."

Field leaders don't just get the information from their sources. They absorb it and feel it themselves. Field leaders live the moment of truth. They practice 'online leadership. They enjoy the moments of execution. They celebrate every intermediate success of the team and magnify it to enhance the morale of the team. They make on-field rectification while facing failures. They can sense the moment of victory or retreat and adopt better damage control plans to minimize the losses.

"Field leaders can experiment with more hit and miss methods due to their pace of response."

Field leaders feel that spending more time in planning can be a sheer waste. They are biased toward the action. They keep a broad outline of the plan in their mind rather than preparing a final blueprint with details of all the nuts and bolts. They feel actions will bring results and reset the strategy. Their focus is on how to make better options work better and produce faster results.

"The presence of the leader at the point of execution provides him an opportunity to refine the strategy based on the field interim review."

Field leaders are also personal trainers to their team members. They observe the strengths and weaknesses of their team members in action. They identify the training needs while the team is in action. They can also promote the right talent after knowing who can produce results.

"Field leaders communicate many things through vibes rather than providing an elaborate explanation."

A paucity of time makes field marshals smarter and faster. They accept things that can quickly get into action and require less implementation time. They are masters of 'quick fix'. They are doers. They focus on doing the right things rather than planning them. They respect the volatility of the environment & trust that their talented team will overcome it rather than a well-thought-out plan.

"Field leaders have more faith in the talent of their team rather than the power of planning and resources."

How to identify leaders with online leadership style? They are gregarious, and always surrounded by people. They crack jokes, speak in a loud voice and also laugh out loud. They are very informal and would hardly follow protocol. They would offer center stage to their talented team member rather than remaining in the limelight always. They are fearless and speak with great conviction. They prefer chatting and joking with the team rather than reading a book or playing piano in solitude.

Offline Leaders: Leaders in Absentia (Board Room Leaders)

Another leadership style is leading the team from the war room. In the case of the corporate world, from the boardroom or the CEOs chamber. They are thinking of animals. they are master planners. They plan to perfection. They plan to the last nut and bolt.

"Followers sing the thoughts of their leader in absentia like prayers."

These leaders provide their unique thought and mission. Their team draws the power from those thoughts and missions. They focus on generating followers for their thoughts. The power of the thoughts provides a virtual presence for offline leaders. Since their physical presence is not the issue, these leaders work with larger audiences.

"Leaders in absentia create a wider ripple which lives longer."

They become the leaders of the masses and work on the long-term vision to achieve their mission. They are revered for years, in some cases even for generations. Their close associates also get their reflected glory. People follow even their associates who lead them using the thoughts of the leader in absentia.

"Wisdom is the mark of offline leaders. They create following through great thoughts."

Leaders in absentia know that wisdom comes from doing different things and not just one specific thing. Their wisdom lays down the processes and policies which become a benchmark for their followers to take routine decisions. They believe that personal experiences can be special cases that happen in a special situation. They think it is impossible to give perfect exposure to the person by planning a simulation. They rather focus on past experiences in the form of case studies.

"Leaders in absentia don't overemphasize their personal experiences. They value their wisdom more than their experiences."

Offline leaders are prudent. They learn from the mistakes of others. They use the experiences of others as case studies. Chanakya in Indian history was one such leader. He wrote a beautiful line which is shown in the picture with his photo.

"Leaders in absentia have a great ability to draw the right inferences."

They don't forget the lessons drawn from the case studies and have an extraordinary ability to leverage those lessons to gain competitive advantages. They develop the strategy based on the inferences drawn from those case studies and develop systems to implement that strategy. MBA education focuses on creating such leaders. MBA education provides them with the opportunity to learn relevant cases. The inferences drawn from case studies become a treasure of such corporate leaders.

"Strategy is an important weapon of offline leaders."

They carefully study the facts and craft their strategy well. Their strategy is well grounded in the inferences drawn from the case studies. They believe in spending enough time on planning. They treat planning time as an investment and not an expense. They undertake a systematic process while preparing the plan. Such leaders have higher patience. They rely heavily on the inputs provided by the field force.

"Offline leaders develop systems that are not person specific."

Such leaders are system driven. Their commitment to systems makes them develop standard operating procedures (SOP) for all business processes. Such SOP becomes the 'good book' of the organization which reflects the leader's wisdom. Their focus is on staff, system, and strategy to achieve the super-ordinate goal. A structure has importance in its way of leadership.

"Leaders in absentia create great organizational structures."

They believe in the authority and responsibility balance. They also create structures with the unity of directions and unity of command. They prefer to recruit the right skills and believe in developing the right style through training. They assume people to possess certain minimum skills and exercise the required style.

"Offline leaders believe that the war can't be won on the field unless it is won on paper."

However, many offline leaders land up winning the war only on paper making them just paper tigers. Plans remain only on paper because of the lack of human skills of these leaders. Their high conceptual skills and administrative skills bear fruits only when they join hands with online leaders who are very strong in technical skills and human relations skills. The doers (offline leaders) can make the planners (offline leaders) very effective and the other way round.

"Offline leaders become very effective when they work alongside online leaders."

In the great Indian mythology, Lord Krishna provided the leadership in absentia. He never touched any arm. He provided wisdom. Arjuna was an online leader who depended on the offline leadership support of Lord Krishna. They had a perfect understanding. When they debated a great book on philosophy was created, Bhagwat Gita became the holy book of Hindus. It is the wisdom shared by the offline leader. It was created to motivate and support the online leader. Together these leaders created history which impacted hundreds of generations. Another example was the pair of Chanakya and Vikramaditya the great. In the case of Mahabharata 'Kauravas' only had field leaders and no offline leader, they failed in their mission.

> *"Offline leaders lead people through the mission, Online leaders reach the mission through people."*

Successful organizations achieve their mission through online and offline leaders. They supplement each other and create a synergetic impact. Both leaders have a few similar but many unique and distinctly different strengths. Offline leaders are high on planning, Online leaders are strong in execution.

> *"Offline leaders are thinking biased, online leaders are action biased. Offline leaders have unique brains, Online leaders have unique hearts."*

The success of the organization depends on how well the offline and online leaders gel. How they rub their shoulders and put them on the organizational wheel. The organization can overcome its inertia only when both, the online and offline leaders, contribute their energies and skills and support the other perspective wholeheartedly.

Leading Flat Organizations

Today, the younger organizations prefer flat organization structures. Are they only taking the lopsided view? What are the challenges involved in leading flat organizations? Leading multi-layered organizations certainly poses a challenge. But leading a flat organization is not easy either. A flat organization can exert power only if it is led by a powerful leader. Such a leader has to be ambidextrous. He is a master of the art of delegation. He inspires his team with a mission. His team has the burning desire to succeed. They are emotionally connected to each other. They have to be 'hands-on' and push each other up. Sharing and caring are their strengths. Flat organizations have to be process driven but they encarve short-cuts very well. Members of the flat organization are high on conceptual skills. They create competitive advantages by looking at the total picture. They would never lose woods for trees. Such flat organizations have lesser inertia, higher agility and better customer centricity.

McKinsey has rightfully identified 'Structure' as an important element of their 7S model along with other S as shown in the figure on the right. In my view, Shared Vision, Strategy and Structure are the important pillars. They support other 4S. 'Structure' determines systems, staff, skills and style. With the change of the structure, those 4 elements have to change drastically. They are specific to the type of structure used by the organization. Changing the structure would lead to changes in the systems, staff, skills and styles. This article is my effort to identify how these 4S would change with a change in the structure. How do systems, staff, skills and style change from the multi-layered, gigantic structure to a flat organization structure?

"The structure of the organization dominates staff, skills and styles of employees and defines the organization culture and values."

Multi-layered, heavy structure organizations Organizations with megastructures have higher penetration. The industry leaders tend to use such structures to encourage specialization and exercise better control. They focus on practising management principles laid down by Henry Fayol, like the division of work, unity of command, authority responsibility relationships, scalar chain etc. Their employees are specialized in different areas and they have different skills. They believe in doing their part well and prefer not to poke into other areas. They have distinct roles with no overlaps. Such organizations have higher resources and they believe in crushing the competition with scale. They exert pressure on their competition through their gigantic size and weight. The flat structure organizations also have certain unique features which are specific to their situation.

Flat organization structures They are popular in fighting organizations. They are younger with a lower average age of employees. They are either challengers or niche players in the industry structure. The 'Style' of flat organizations is radically different from multi-layered. Specialization is promoted by multi-layered organizations. Their specialists protect the organizations by digging trenches and taking defensive positions. Flat organizations train employees who can wield swords in both hands. The offence is the best defence, is the style of flat organizations.

"Multi-layered organizations focus on defence whereas flat organizations take offensive stance."

Usually, flat organizations are led by great leaders who are hands-on, higher risk takers, fearless and very swift in their response. For them, their team is the best asset they have. They lead through their team. They are choosy in selecting people. They know one rotten apple can spoil the whole basket. Their focus during the selection is on value fitment, coachability, agility, tenacity to perform under pressure, empathetic attitude, ability to work in a team and multi-tasking ability.

"Leaders of the flat organizations are possessive about recruitment. They would never delegate recruitment."

Great leaders handling flatter organization structures provide higher importance to human resources (HR). They believe HR to be everybody's job. They believe that specialization brings down productivity. They prefer outsourcing jobs with specialization. They have a higher commitment to training their team. They happily perform the job of the coach and become part of the training team. They also believe in job rotations and refuse to keep roles specific to persons.

"Leaders of flat organizations want their team members to be 'the jack of everything and master of one'."

Leaders of flat organizations select their team members who have leadership potential. They encourage task-specific leaders. They look at the task as projects and expect different employees to lead different projects. They want everybody to be the leader in a specific job. Leaders of flat organizations provide great importance to opportunity and exposure. They are courageous and do not hesitate to assign a critical job to a young team member. William Wallace, a leader of Scotland successfully led a flat organization. Along with Andrew Moray, Wallace defeated an English army at the Battle of Stirling Bridge in September 1297.

"Flat organizations are 'leadership factories' due to the decentralization of leadership, opportunity, exposure and coaching by the leader himself."

The members of the team get training on the art of delegation. They are taught how to delegate but still support the activity by remaining hands-on. They learn the importance of empowering others by sharing their skills & resources in order to maintain the focus of the organization on the mission. They realize how their personal agenda gets served when they prioritize & achieve the organizational agenda.

> *"Leaders of flat organizations use tactics as a cutting-edge tool & out-fox their competition"*

Chhatrapati Shivaji Maharaj escaped from the prison which was surrounded by hundreds of armed guards using tactics that the enemy couldn't think of. He routed his escape through boxes of sweets. (As shown in the picture). The leaders of flat organizations know that the edge of the sword of strategy is tactics. They spend a great amount of time deciding 'how to do it' after deciding 'what to do'.

> *"Using innovative tactics is a mark of the flat organizations. They nullify the competitors' strategy with innovative tactics."*

Employees in flat organizations are young and coachable. They have multi-tasking ability; hence they can remain hands-on & fill up the gap when their co-worker is on leave or on tour. They form stronger bonds; hence, they are comfortable in delegation & empowerment. Their age provides them energy and confidence. They can blend work and personal life better. They spend an hour for their personal needs during office hours but compensate for it by spending multiple hours of personal time, even on vacation for attending to urgent & important priorities at work.

> *"Employees who worked for layered organizations find it difficult to work with a flat organization & other way round."*

For the employees who worked with multi-layered structures, promotion means handling many more people and being in charge of a department with a lot of authority. They see promotion as an opportunity to wield power. But the perspective of the employees in the flat organization is different. For them, the world is the same even after promotion. For them, promotion means higher pay & perks.

"In flat organizations, promotion is a responsibility rather than an authority."

Dealing with the cultural shock Indian industry is witnessing many start-ups. These start-ups maintain flat structures and attract young talent. This article can be useful to young professionals who are planning to join start-ups. It would also ring a bell for the seasoned professionals who spent their life in multi-layered organizations and thinking of taking key positions in start-ups which have flat structures.

In nutshell, I have a message for the recruiters, HR persons and corporate executives. There exist radical differences in the profile, values, culture, skills and style of the employees who work for multi-layered organizations & flat structure organizations. One group is from Mars and the other is from Venus. They are acclimated to their own organizational cultures and customs which are the outcome of structures. They are from different planets. Required care is to be taken in the recruitment, selection, Training and orientation of employees who come from different organizational structures. Employees who worked for the market leader usually find it difficult to work with the challenger or niche player and employee who worked for the challenger or niche player feels restricted and suffocated when he starts a career with the market leader.

CHAPTER THIRTEEN

Status Quo Leadership

Under some special situations, a few managers, who are followers, are appointed as leaders. They know self-limitations, for sure. Such 'nominated leaders' always fear change and they struggle to maintain the status quo. They know very well that they can be drowned in change. Status quo leaders always project that their organization has reached its peak. (Published on LinkedIn on 4 August 2017. Got 105 Likes; 11 Comments and 87 Shares)

"A leader who loves the status quo soon becomes a follower - John Maxwell"

In fact, under some special situations, a few managers, who are followers, are appointed as leaders. They know self-limitations, for sure. Such 'nominated leaders' always fear change and they struggle to maintain the status quo. They know very well that they can be drowned in change. Status quo leaders always project that their organization has reached its peak. They try hard to carve out a segment to indicate that their organization is the leader. Status quo leaders make tall claims about the leadership of their company in a specific segment of the Industry. For a few of them don't forget to add a disclaimer, at the bottom, in the smallest possible font size, explaining the micro category in which they survive and lead.

"'Status quo leaders' focus on the 'due diligence approach to management."

Status quo leaders identify processes and systems which lead to their elevation and try to establish them as a norm. Thereafter, their focus is on due diligence. They design various formats to monitor their control. The employees are required to submit the reports at a regular frequency. Some positions are created to follow up and monitor the preparation of such reports. In due course, the monitoring authority forgets the purpose of the report. They fail to alter the report formats to suit the changing context.

"Status quo leadership makes the organization 'report oriented' rather than 'task oriented'"

Some reports are never analyzed by anyone but the employees are required to submit those reports religiously. The reports and the reporting system become as sacred as the holy Bible. A status quo leader identifies the control levers and prepares a dashboard. The senior team members are required to make and submit the dashboard. The leader forgets that the dashboard is just an effect and the cause lies in deficient leadership and management. Only convenient inferences are drawn from the poor dashboard parameters. Measures initiated for rectification are targeted toward protecting the leadership position rather than correcting the damage.

"Formats and deadlines are most sacrosanct under 'status quo leadership'."

The biggest sin of an employee could be either non-submission of the report or submission of the 'nil report'. He is safe when the columns are filled in. Nil report is reviewed seriously. The Key Result Area (KRA) of an employee is dominated by the types of reports he needs to produce. It is dictated by the deadlines for the submission of those reports. Employees get bog-down by the reports. Timely form filling becomes their main profession.

"Status quo leader drives the organization by the reports rather than the mission."

Employees ensure that no column remains blank in the structured/printed report format. They plan their activity smartly around the format of the report. I have seen many tourists busy taking snaps or in video shooting the scenic beauty rather than enjoying it during their visit. Similarly, employees in the status quo organization become busier with report production than result production.

"The 'Status quo leaders' transform leadership into governance. A leader becomes a regulator."

There is a great emphasis on the audit function. Over-meticulous audit suffocates the employees. Small deviations are zoomed up. Auditors dictate terms to line managers. Such power transfer demoralizes the performers. Employees lose autonomy. They fear using their discretions. Any team player who has a different view is considered a 'trouble trigger'. sycophants start bothering performers. Insecure leadership supports sycophants.

"Status quo leader fosters mediocracy & sycophancy. He develops an informal organization within the organization."

The leader develops an informal organization for protecting his personal interest. Such an informal organization runs parallel to the formal organization. Organization within an organization complicates decision-making. The designations become misleading. The employees in a higher grade may not be as powerful as the members of the informal organization who work officially in the lower grade. The reporting system, deadlines, and auditing encroach and dominate the work culture.

> **"Employees develop a minimalistic attitude under a status quo leader."**

The work culture suppresses creativity, initiative, and healthy competition. Employees work for the targets. They resist a lot while formulating targets. They don't provide 100%. Even good employees develop a minimalistic approach. They don't stretch themselves and their performance targets. The performers either quit or keep a low profile. Status quo leaders forget that change is the only constant. They forget that they have to keep running fast. A stand-still organization, like an asleep lion, is a soft target for competitors and poachers.

> **"Maintaining Status Quo in Market Leadership Like the individual leadership, the market leadership has to be dynamic. The market leader should not try to maintain the status quo."**

The market leader has to initiate the change and lead the change.

Bajaj Auto was the market leader in the Indian scooter industry with more than three fourth of the market share. In the 1970s, they had more than a decade-long waiting list of customers who paid full money, booked a scooter, and were waiting for the delivery of the scooter. The popular scooter model, 'Bajaj Chetak', was available only if customers paid in US dollars.

> **"The market leader shouldn't assume that they reached the peak and sleep on their laurels."**

Bajaj did not work on product up-gradation and modification. They kept launching models only with cosmetic changes and ignored customer complaints. Bajaj thought they were maintaining the status quo in the scooter segment while they were doing a wonderful job in the motorcycle segment. In early 2000, Honda launched their scooter model, 'Activa', in the Indian market. Activa became the market leader only in 3 years. Bajaj had to stop scooter production & they had to change their focus to motorcycles. They set an apt example of blowing up the market leadership by trying to maintain the status quo through inaction. Recently, the Indian two-wheeler market is tilting in favor of scooters. Bajaj is still maintaining the status quo. This time they are ignoring an important shift in customer preferences. They are not launching scooters. Maruti Suzuki which is the market leader in the Indian car market has achieved almost 50% market share. But they are not prepared to maintain the status quo. Maruti Suzuki is still trying hard to increase the market share.

"Remaining hungry for growth is the only way to maintain the leadership position."

Maruti Suzuki has learnt its lesson from Bajaj. They fight the war every day. They try to block every strong move by their competitors. There are many examples of status quo leaders losing the leadership. Nokia was the leader in the India mobile handset market. Colgate commanded a very high market share in the Indian tooth care market but lost considerable market share. Samsung dislodged Nokia from the leadership position but later became victim to other mobile companies from India and China. Smart leaders know very well that:

"It is harder to maintain leadership than to acquire it."

Some leading brands believe that once they achieve the scale they should focus on profitability. They try to cut corners. They go easy on the spending on marketing and product development. They start believing that defending is easier than launching an attack. They assume that their competitors need to spend much more and they need not worry about matching competitors' promotional budgets. But the smart brands like Coke, McDonald's, and Maruti Suzuki have learned their marketing lessons well. They know, 'out of sight is out of mind'. They know that 'attack is the only way to defend'.

CHAPTER FOURTEEN

Quasi Leadership

Quasi-leaders look like leaders. They have many features of leaders but for a few critical ones. Mission, chemistry with the team, uniqueness of characters like glamour and grace, caliber & talent, support of the gut, and public relation (PR) skills could be the missing links between quasi-leaders and leaders. Quasi-leaders rise to leadership stature because they are at right the right place at the right time. Usually, they become leaders after some great leaders who are too possessive and don't do succession planning. Some leaders initially appear like quasi-leaders but eventually mature as roaring tigers. How do such quasi-leaders lead? What legacy did they leave and how to deal with such leaders if you are their followers? (Published on LinkedIn on 25 April 2018. Got 256 Likes; 38 Comments and 63 Shares)

Do you recollect the childhood bedtime story of a donkey who wearing the skin of a lion threatened other animals in the jungle? The donkey could do it until a fox identified the truth. In the corporate jungle, there are enough people who pretend to be a leader. I call them 'Quasi-leaders'.

'Quasi-leaders look like leaders. They have many features of leaders but for a few critical ones. Mission, chemistry with the team, uniqueness of characters like glamour and grace, caliber and talent, support of the gut, and public relation (PR) skills could be the missing links between quasi-leaders and leaders. Quasi-leaders don't know what they are up to. They neither have a sense of direction nor do they have a compass. This handicap prevents them from developing a vision. Quasi-leaders can't see tomorrow. Usually, they are the 'imposed leaders'. They get into leadership positions due to inheritance, family stature, or proximity to a great leader. They could also be among those lucky folks who were selected as assistants by the great leaders, but due to the unexpected early demise of the leader, they get into the leadership saddle. Quasi-leaders rise to leadership stature because they are at right the right place at the right time. Usually, they become leaders after some great leaders who are too possessive and don't do succession planning. Some leaders initially appear like quasi-leaders but eventually mature as roaring tigers. How do such quasi-leaders lead? What legacy did they leave and how to deal with such leaders if you are their follower in the official capacity?

Sometimes we wonder how somebody got into the leadership position when he or she doesn't have the required caliber, acceptance, mission and vision, and also charisma. They are the products of unique situations. Such people have few competitive advantages. Their long association with the organization is supported by their loyalty. They may not work smarter but they work harder. They log in more hours, pile up leaves, and are seen more in the office. They don't use a watch, reach the office before time and stay until the shutters are pulled down. Such people focus on hard work, loyalty, and sincerity. They avoid confrontations because they don't take a firm stand on sensitive issues. Team members don't have anything 'for or against' them. Their rise to leadership positions surprises the team. Their team neither expects nor is prepared for their leadership. I refer to such leaders as 'quasi-leaders'. They look like leaders but seriously lack many critical qualities of the leader.

"Great leaders are chosen. Quasi-leaders are imposed. They are products of environment. They are at right place at right time."

They believe that the route to leadership is through the longevity of service, loyalty, and proximity to the boss, They don't belong to a team though they create informal organization out of their insecurity. They believe strategy and planning hardly help. They look at tactics as dirty politics. While great leaders hold their mission on the top, retaining the power and position becomes a mission of the quasi-leaders. Great leaders look at leadership as a responsibility,

"Followers get hooked to great leaders because of the hope leaders create through their commitment to mission, and ability to attract resources."

Great Leaders, Great Perspective Great leaders trust concave lenses because their sight is set on the long-term & train their people to use convex lenses so that they get into meticulous planning and execution to ensure operational effectiveness and efficiency. Their focus is on how to create wealth that provides long-term benefits to a larger audience.

"Great leaders create wealth by focusing on the mission. Quasi Leaders are obsessed about earning quarterly profits by focusing on the short term objectives."

Great leaders' footprints are their perceptions & perspective. They understand things in a much more positive way. When in a particular situation people complain about a problem, they smell opportunity. When people fear a threat they get excited about an opportunity wrapped in that threat. Their perspective toward business is radically different.

"Quasi-leaders look at profits as an objective. The great leaders look at profit as a resource to create tomorrow, to achieve their mission."

Profit is never a bad word for great leaders but their perspective is different. They are more concerned about ongoing profits. Their concern is about the profits of the customers and partners. Great leaders are wise people. They know, they can't win if their customers lose, they can't win if their suppliers lose. They know they can grow only with their people. Their perspective of 'their people' is broader. It includes all the stakeholders. Great leaders are worried about investors' money more than their own.

"Great leaders never kill hen for golden eggs."

Investors know the obsession of the great leaders to provide them returns & the amount of care they take to provide security to the investors. Whenever such leaders launch a public issue, it gets oversubscribed many more times. Quasi-leaders are desperate to prove their worth. Great leaders believe in developing their character before developing a career. Their character is a set of values that are very dear to them as is their passion. Their mission emerges out of their set of values and passion. Their 'vision' is to re-orient the world to suit their passion. This orientation develops leaders' perspectives. Those who share their vision and re-orient themselves as per the leaders' perspective join the leaders to help them succeed in the mission and see their vision as reality.

"The noble intentions and perspective of the great leaders develops loyal soldiers."

Clarity of thoughts and direction, sharp perception, unique perspective, and noble intentions are the steps in the leadership ladder. Quasi-leaders try to jump these steps & face the music. Great leaders know very well that if they care for people then people will share their mission. They are very choosy about selecting every member of their team. They also spend a lot of time training the team. Having done these fundamental things right they don't hesitate to delegate. They know that only delegation can give required exposure and opportunity to perform. Quasi-leaders don't have such a high level of commitment to people and hence their followers are only 'sycophants' with a short-term personal agenda.

"The great leaders develop a team and delegate 'today'. They focus on creating tomorrow. Quasi-leaders struggle managing 'today'."

Great leaders: Work for tomorrow, delegate today Great leaders do not get bogged down in 'today'. They always discuss great ideas. Their 'vision' helps them in seeing tomorrow and hence they are called visionary. They want people to see how the world will look like when their mission is accomplished. They stay in a virtual world. They want to change the world. Great leaders treat the status quo not only as a monotony but also as a sin. They feel it is underemployment and talent should not be deployed in maintaining the status quo.

> *"Great leaders are excited about the change, quasi leaders are obsessed about status quo."*

Great leaders are change agents. They know that only talented people have the competency to bring innovation and change and hence they are talent biased. Quasi-leaders hardly gel well with talented employees. They feel such employees are pampered, complacent, and lack loyalty. Inability to handle talent repels talented employees from quasi-leaders who are then left with mediocre employees.

> *"Great leaders are talent hunters. They have a natural instinct to identify talent. They know how to train the talent for tomorrow."*

Quasi-leaders don't get attracted to talent because they don't chase excellence. Most of them are not even aware of the excellence. They get nervous when they see glittering talent. According to quasi-leaders excellence is a luxury, a hypothetical proposition, and also a fad. They develop a defense mechanism against excellence. They prepare their version of likely problems associated with pursuing excellence.

> *"Great leader takes out fears of his people, quasi-leader installs fear & uses it as a weapon to establish the power."*

How do the quasi-leaders lead? Once they grab the power they operate differently. Their methods, tools, and processes are different from those of great leaders. Their approach is minimalistic. They will ensure that things will be done as per the system's requirement but shall not travel the extra mile to improve the system.

"The minimalistic approach of quasi-leaders breed mediocracy in the organization."

They lead by due diligence. For them, systems are more important than the business. 'Auditor satisfaction' gets precedence over 'customer satisfaction'. For them, the 'audit report' is more important than the 'performance report'. Such leaders fear change. They feel their grip may get lost because of the change. They may get changed with the change.

"In the era of quasi-leaders, auditors become more powerful than the line managers."

Leading by Creating & Sharing Energies Due to the unhealthy perception & perspective of quasi-leaders the team members do not give them their energy. Because of this attitude of not putting in 100%, the organization suffers.

"Under quasi-leaders, people work harder but not smarter. They work efficiently but not effectively."

The team spends more time on maintaining due diligence and reports in the given format. The organization loses its innovative edge in the marketplace. It becomes 'systems driven' rather than 'customer driven'. Such due diligence leaders can also be called 'tick-mark' leaders. They identify key result areas (KRA) and ensure bare minimum performance in every element of KRA so that there is a tick mark in front of every element instead of a blank. They project an 'all is well' situation. Their obsession is formats and deadlines. They don't want to leave any questions unanswered. But they need pre-cooked alternatives. They don't trigger any trouble. They enjoy a smooth ride. Those who create energies have to create friction and heat. They lead by creating a sense of purpose not only in the profession but also in the personal lives of their team members.

"Quasi-leaders consume resources. Great leaders generate resources, create energies much more than the resources they consume."

How to deal with Quasi-leaders? The insecure mind of the quasi-leaders makes them very difficult people to deal with. Quasi-leaders look at talented employees as competitors and are constantly in the hunt for the weaknesses of talented employees. A few suggestions to deal with them are as follows:

Outlive them When quasi-leaders hijack the organizations, most of the good people feel suffocated and they start leaving the organization. Those who couldn't locate a good job get into their own shell and stop sharing their energies with their teams. Never resign to help the cause of quasi-leaders. The most difficult task is to outlive the quasi-leader. But those who do it successfully reap the benefits.

Don't punish the organization The team members don't support the team with full energy. This results in organizational loss and also personal loss. One has to ensure not to get demoralized. Maintaining morale and boosting the morale of other team members is the only solution. In fact, one should perform better so that quasi-leaders may not have anything against you.

When they go low, you go high Avoid hitting below the belt. If they go low, you go high. Graceful behavior is always rewarded.

Wait for the right opportunity Wait for the right opportunity. Use the time to improve relationships with other people in the organization.

Quasi-leaders could be beneficiaries of a tussle between various factions in the organization. Sometimes there is a deadlock in an organization. It is an outcome of a fight between two strong informal groups that can't grab the power themselves but don't let others grab it. In such a deadlock, quasi-leaders may get benefited. They become leaders by filtering consensus through the process of elimination. Some quasi-leaders are just 'In-charge leaders' who hold the leadership charge due to the unexpected departure of the great leader. Poor succession planning results in the appointment of the quasi-leaders. They are given a charge as a stop-gap arrangement but it gets extended beyond a limit due to the lack of consensus.

CHAPTER FIFTEEN

Training the Traits

hen we lose important battles against our competition despite giving our 100%, then remember that traits played the difference. For the final attack, we need to set our team as per their traits, train them well, and make them develop their own software. (Published on LinkedIn on 29 July 2017. Got 88 Likes; 11 Comments and 86 Shares.)

How are the great performers manufactured?

"If you want to be the best, you have to do things that other people aren't willing to do." Michael Phelps.

He was diagnosed with attention deficit hyperactivity disorder (ADHD) at the age of 9. He started learning swimming, very reluctantly, at 7, on his mother's insistence. His elder sister, Whitney, was a champion swimmer. He learned swimming out of sibling rivalry and also sibling motivation. At 15, he was the youngest American athlete ever to participate in the Olympics. At 31, he was the oldest American swimmer to get the gold medal in Olympics swimming. He played in 5 Olympics and won 28 medals (23 gold medals shown in the above photo) and set 39 world records in swimming. Michael Phelps is a performer of the highest order by any standards. Why could only Phelps do it? What did he do that nobody else was prepared to do?

> *"Great performances are the outcome of identifying world-class traits and imparting state-of-the-art training to them."*

Bob Bowman, the trainer of Michael Phelps for the last 20 years, says that when Michael came to him he had genes and a body suitable for swimming. He has a long torso and short legs. This helped him to reduce the resistance of his body to water. His humongous set of feet is attached to extremely flexible ankles, which work like fins (similar to a shark). Athletes often envy Phelps because it has been scientifically proven that his body produces only half the lactic acid that his rivals need to handle. This significantly reduces his recovery time and he can get ready for the next round of swimming faster than anybody else. Additionally, he hardly gets stiff muscles or any other muscular problems because of his genetics. Phelps has huge palms, which helps his paddling capacity. (Courtesy: https://www.scienceabc.com). Those were his traits. He had the genes of a great swimmer. His body was unique and the most suited to swimming. When something outstanding is achieved in the world then it is always a combination of natural and human elements. Natural elements are God's gift. Human elements are diligently developed through training and practice.

> *"Natural elements are the hardware of success and human elements are the software."*

The harder part is developing this software. God alone makes the hardware but it needs a team to develop such software. The player, the coach, the team, support staff, cheerleaders, and fans make the team. Michael's elder sisters were his cheerleaders. They attended most of his top matches and cheered him. The components of the software are Passion Although Michael started swimming reluctantly at a very young age, it became his passion. He never gave up on it. I quote Michael here: "I found something I love and never gave up" Henry Ford once said, "Give me a man who sings on his job." Michael is that man. He enjoyed his work. He became a fish and enjoyed his stay in the water very much. He is in the water for at least six hours and swims for around 13 miles every day. He once said, "I feel most at home in the water. I disappear. That's where I belong."

Focus Michael remained focused and never diluted his focus. For swimming, he traveled to all parts of America and also many parts of the world. He said a funny thing: "People say to me, You're so lucky. You get to see the world. But I don't. I go to the hotel and the pools and back again. THAT'S IT." Michael clearly knew his focus he never went on sight-seeing trips, anywhere, when he went to play matches. He had a purpose and he stuck to it. Goal Orientation Bob admitted that he never saw anybody as goal-oriented as Michael. In Michael's own words:

> *"The more you dream the farther you get."*

Consistency and Hard work Before securing the initial Olympic medals he worked consistently for 6 years for 365 days a year. He also practiced on his birthdays and on Christmas. When he was not well, he took medicines and swam. *He had no holidays.* Discipline Bob told that Michael went to him when he was 11. He was an amazing swimmer for his age but lacked discipline. Bob identified that weakness and they jointly worked on that weakness. Self Actualization Michael never did anything to earn fame or money. He got into self-actualization mode. He described what swimming meant to him: "I want to test my maximum and see how much I can do. And

I want to change the world of swimming." One can draw corporate lessons from Michael's life story. Students can also learn many things from him and through his success.

Career Lesson

We must identify our traits. God has given feathers to birds, fins to fish, and nails and teeth to a tiger. He gives something to everyone so that we can use it, develop it and make our living out of it.

"We will have a huge advantage in today's competitive world if we develop our careers around our traits."

Remember, traits are just hardware. We need to develop the software. Passion, focus, consistency, goal orientation, discipline, hard work, and self-actualization are required to be developed by us. Nobody else can do it for us. We have to work out ourselves if we want to remain fit.

"A career is like fitness, can't be delegated completely."

However, we will have to find our trainer. Michael identified the right trainer and swam for him for his entire life. Bob Bowman said he spent 90% of his life on Phelps. He was always on the board near him when Michael was in the water. Finding such teachers is difficult. Only lucky people get such crazy teachers who give up their life for yours. Many people approach me for advice on their careers. They want to know how they identify their passion. I ask them three questions: What do you do on your vacation? Tell me one thing that you want to do so desperately that you will pay money for letting you do that. What does your girlfriend/boyfriend like the most about you? My advice would then connect their responses to these three questions. Corporate Lessons from Michael Phelp's Mega Success While working in organizations we must remember the concept of traits. Both genders have certain traits. We should not ignore them under gender equality. When we say gender equality we mean 'gender social equality. The respect and status of both genders must be the same. They should not be discriminated against only for their gender. Every team must have a good combination of men and women. But we must understand the traits and distribute the work accordingly. Traits may not be gender specific. These days most of the traits are uni-gender. We must identify the traits of a person and allocate the job. This should be done only when it is most required and we are up against very difficult tasks, like winning an Olympic medal. For normal, routine work is highly unnecessary and can create friction among the team members. When we say that we should not leave a single stone unturned, this should be the last stone which you must turn.

"When we lose important battles against our competition despite giving our 100%, then remember that traits played the difference."

For the final attack, we need to set our team as per their traits, train them well, and make them develop their own software. When the team wins, the trainer wins, the cheerleaders win and the fans win.

From Crown to Captaincy: Transforming Leadership Game

s the jobs are transforming into careers, boundaries between the workplace and home are vanishing. Offices are getting embedded in homes as the 'work from home' concept propagates. Millennials, the young leaders in their 30s (born after the year 1980) are changing the leadership game. These young leaders are keeping the crown aside and wearing the captaincy cap. The leaders are evolving as captains. An increasing number of corporate leaders are looking at leadership as a responsibility rather than a position. (Published on LinkedIn on 14 August 2018. Got 168 Likes; 25 Comments and 7 Shares)

My generation worked under bosses who were 'English-Indians'. This is a new term I have coined like Indian-Americans or African-Americans or Chinese-Americans etc. These English-Indian bosses were very much Indians but were highly inspired by the style of the administration used traditionally by the British while ruling India. Their leadership style was unique. Some of the features of this 'Angrej (a term used by common Indians for the British) style of leadership' were as follows:

"The leader's wish was the command the team. He couldn't be questioned or challenged for any decision."

The leader was supreme. The leader was always put before the team. The team had to follow the leader. These leaders wanted 'hands' rather than 'brains'. Loyalty was defined as the ability of the subordinate to mindlessly follow the leader and obey all of his wishes & not just commands. The leader was put on a pedestal.

"The delegation was restricted to responsibility and authority remained the leader's privilege."

Team players used to be very happy if the leader delegated some responsibility to them. However, all the decision-making authorities always remained with the leader and the subordinate had to take his advice on all minor elements of the work. The leader's absence used to put everything at a standstill mode. The leaders loved to see the decisions getting piled up in their absence. The higher the pile bigger was the leader's satisfaction. The leader's office was a war-room, decisions were taken there. It was below the leader's dignity to work in the field. They isolated themselves under the pretext of the protocol. Our leaders had a 'work from office' culture. They would always be busy in the internal meetings, analyzing the options and making decisions for every team member. The leader's field visit was the big event. They were supposed to come to the field only for inaugurations or on protocol visits.

"The informal organizations were more powerful than the formal organizations"

The leader was always surrounded by sycophants. They were the 'gatekeepers' who controlled access to the leader. They influenced the leader. Our leaders could hear their whispers and were deaf to yelling by other employees or customers. These sycophants summoned anyone irrespective of their position in the hierarchy. These were the true power centers that created the second axis on the power map.

> *"Formality, protocol, due diligence, and code of conduct were the most sacrosanct words and actions"*

Our leaders were formal and protocol-driven. Their focus was systems requirements & compliance to the last detail. The policy was the holy book. They expected us to maintain a code of conduct laid down to maintain their position. We had to seek their appointment after checking their moods with the secretary. If we had to write some notes to the super seniors at the head office then we had to type it in MS Word & forward it to the bosses' email. His secretary would 'copy' & 'paste' it as a message from him, under his name & would mail it from his e-mail account. Sending any direct mails from the branch office to the head office was seen as an attempt of bypassing or trace-passing. Bosses developed the art to demonstrate their distinct position & superiority over subordinates. They developed different tools, methods, protocols & policies to help them in asserting their power, They would drink tea in a royal tea set while others were given cheap paper cups.

From Boss to Leader: Evolution of the Indian Professionals Many of my students are now in a leadership positions. I have been advising Indian companies in Marketing & business development, I can feel the difference millennial brought in the leadership game.

> *"The young Indian leaders are distinctly different in their attitudes. They embrace responsibility and delegating authority. Today's captains are field marshals. They plan on moving rather than spending hours in the boardrooms."*

They behave like 'Captains' rather than 'Kings'. Young leaders, today, are much more mature and secure. They can digest the power in a much better fashion than our bosses. Our bosses boasted power, the young leaders hid it nicely. Our bosses used power as an ornament, and young leaders use it as a tool but very sparingly. Our bosses looked at it as a position, young leaders look at it as a role. These captains can't escape from the team player's role. Young leaders never use double standards. They know that they have to contribute and add value as leaders. They know that they need to be good followers if they expect others to follow them. They get merged into the team and don't have an obsession to maintain a distinct identity. Their performance is their identity. They stand out by their performance rather than the attire of the Emperor. They prove their superiority by outperforming the team members in the same environment & on similar parameters. Young leaders set higher performance standards through their own performance rather than using the leadership position as an excuse to get exempted from personal targets. These captains influence their team by demonstrating personal performance and raising the bar for everyone. They get accepted as leaders due to their ability to add value. They also demonstrate an ability to shoulder extra responsibility of the captaincy over and above their role as a team player. As products and services are maturating days by day, the captains are getting younger and younger. These young leaders are more humble, open, transparent, objective, talent biased, techno-savvy, upright, and focused. They are omnipresent in their organization rather than omnipotent. They prefer managing by 'moving around' rather than getting en-shackled in mega office chambers. They are always there for their team whenever the team needs them. They hate wielding power and share it with others by decentralization and delegation. They believe in empowering rather than controlling subordinates. They don't mind accepting other captains for the other games or for the different formats of the game. Today a principal has to be a good teacher. The dean has to lead the team of academicians by maintaining his own research & publication record. Dwyane Wade has pressure to perform as a player because he leads 'Miami heat', the NBA basketball team with players like Lebron James and Bush. Dhoni leads the Indian cricket team with talents like Virat and Rahul.

Millennial leaders are re-writing the leadership dictionary. The word 'Boss' is giving way to a 'Senior'. They don't have 'subordinates' (a person under the authority or control of another within an organization) but have 'associates'. (a partner or companion at work).

They don't 'employ' someone but they take the help of somebody in their businesses.

They guide rather than criticize. They share the area of improvement rather than highlighting weaknesses. In the case of our bosses, the subordinates had to 'request' and the bosses had to 'approve'. The young managers prefer the word 'consent' or 'concurrence'. ***They 'advice' rather than 'direct'.***

> *"Millennials know very well that their display of anger has a high cost. The demoralized employees can be a liability."*

Better Anger Management. Millennials are careful with their anger. They know that the best way to demoralize any employee is to display anger. When they are angry they get into silent mode or say, "I am not happy." Their team can listen to their silence.

What is fuelling this transformation? The roots of the polished & humane approach of young leaders can be related to many things.

> *"Millennials don't have a deprived mindset. Their upbringing in abundance makes them feel secure."*

Earlier generations in India faced a scarcity of resources. Limited pocket money, limited seats for admissions into educational institutes, limited jobs, limited business opportunities, etc. Generations before the 1980s developed a 'scarcity mindset'. They had to share everything with their siblings, cousins, family & friends due to limited resources. It affected their ability to share anything with others easily.

> *"'Forced sharing' developed possessive nature"*

Sharing, delegation, transparency, openness, and candid feedback were rare qualities. Post-1980s the number of children per family in India reduced. Mothers also started earning salaries. The service sector emerged strongly creating a positive impact on the salary structures. The salaried people & salaries, both, increased many folds. The disposable income of families increased. The regular and assured monsoon facilitated rich agriculture and hence affluence in rural India. Prosperous India provided happy childhood with abundance. Millennials were brought up in a different environment than their earlier generations. Westernization also created a deep impact on them. This westernized generation nicely blended the management culture of the West with the Indian culture. I am witness to the professional development of Millenials. I taught them in their MBA, provided them consultancy and advice on business development, and trained them in corporate jobs. I am very positive about the future of the Indian corporate sector because I know that it is in the safe hands of talented, hard-working, globalized Indian Millenials who will definitely make it bigger than the earlier generations.

CHAPTER SEVENTEEN

From Deputy to Chief – A journey of Thousand Miles

Becoming the Deputy need not be the last step toward the chief's chair. Why do most of the deputies exhaust their stamina and fail to move on to the top slot? Do they lack some of the leadership skills required by the chief? Many times the deputy is selected on parameters that are radically different from the parameters necessary for the chief's position. (Published on LinkedIn on 26 April 2017. Got 42 Likes; 5 Comments and 41 Shares).

Interestingly, only 4 out of 48 Vice-Presidents of America went on to become Presidents at the end of their tenure as vice presidents. In India, out of 7 deputy prime ministers, nobody became the prime minister during the next tenure, and out of 12 vice presidents, not even half of them became the president.

"The journey to the chief's office does not necessarily go through the deputy's office."

Becoming the Deputy need not be the last step toward the chief's chair. Why do most of the deputies exhaust their stamina and fail to move on to the top slot? Do they lack some of the leadership skills required by the chief? Many times the deputy is selected on parameters that are radically different from the parameters necessary for the chief's position. Usually, the chief chooses the deputy. The personal choice of the chief is critical in the process. They are possessive of their team members and the relationship they share with them.

"The chief tends to over-emphasize personal chemistry while selecting the deputy. He tends to choose his assistant rather than the successor."

Some chiefs tend to look at the potential candidates for the deputy's position as a threat. Their primary concern would be their tenure rather than their succession. They do not want an over-ambitious deputy who could trigger trouble for them. They love their deputy leaving the final decision and veto power to them. Independent deputies tend to make decisions and take concurrence from the Chief. But some chiefs love to provide 'consent' or 'approval' rather than just a concurrence.

Growing organically in any organization is like playing the 'snake & ladder' game. One gets the support of many ladders, on the way up. But there is always a danger of snakes. As indicated in the adjoining picture, the highest threat is to the second last position. One can be thrown down from 99th house to 6th in no time. Professional deputy tries to delegate the micro-management to their team. He develops alternatives and emphasizes his strong recommendation of a specific solution. Some chiefs do not like this style. They want to know the details rather than just alternatives. Some chiefs also get into micro-management. The chief tends to question the delegation done by the deputy. They love to delegate the job themselves. They have their own reasons for the same. They may not share those reasons with their deputy. In case the deputy does it then they feel that the deputy is stepping over their foot. It creates friction between the deputy and the chief. Deputy must avoid a conflict with the chief. He can only be the loser. The heat of friction can loosen his grip. The chief is on the last lap of his career but the deputy has not yet begun his journey hence the risk lies only with the Deputy and the chief has nothing to lose.

"The deputy depends on the chief for the decision, and hence they are being looked down on by their team."

The team expects the deputy to make a prompt decision and get the concurrence of the chief in due course. Chief wants it to be discussed with him before the decision is made. Thus the deputy gets caught between the devil and the deep sea. Some chiefs do not hesitate to change the decision taken by the deputy. They might call subordinates and probe. They establish direct communication with subordinates and bypass the deputy. Usually, delegation and empowerment start at the level below the deputy. Such behavior of the chief brings embarrassment to the deputy. His reaction pattern becomes critical. If he fails to handle such a situation then he becomes a pawn, loses importance and the team bypasses him on many occasions reporting directly to the chief. The longer tenure of the chief brings permanent disability to the deputy. He gets so much used to the protection and bossing that he loses the ability to function independently.

"Smart deputy waits for his turn. Becomes indispensable by adding value"

Smart deputy identifies the weaknesses of the chief and develops himself in those areas. By doing so he starts adding value which earns respect for him. He learns to put the chief to work. He exploits the chief's problems to his advantage. He snatches the work & power from the chief by working harder and smarter. He generates time by working an extra hour. He uses opportunities generated by the chief's absence and a paucity of time.

"Smart deputy creates informal organization and becomes virtual chief well before he gets that position formally."

He develops a humane approach. Goes easy with his team. Adds value to their work. Coaches them well. Supports them whenever they need it the most. He protects the team members from the wrath of the chief. He uses the ladder of the human relationship to overcome the snake's powers of the chief.

> *"Smart deputy learns the art of bowing his own trumpet without the chief noticing it."*

Piggy Back Management: Some chiefs use their deputy for unpleasant jobs. They do piggyback when there is a chance of spoiling human relations or some other personal risk. They train deputies to play the 'good cop- bad cop' game. Naturally, the deputy becomes a bad cop and attracts the wrath of the team. It creates problems for the deputy while becoming the chief. It is assumed that the deputy gets 'the first right to reject' the chief's position. But the fact is exactly the opposite.

> *"Usually, the deputy becomes the chief only as a last resort."*

The statistics given in the opening paragraph attests above claim. Being deputy one needs to play second fiddle. But the fiddler who plays second fiddle hardly gets the recognition and respect he deserves. Deputy needs to demonstrate many of the soldier's skills & simultaneously learn the general's skills. They have to remember that they would be general one day. That day can be tomorrow. They should try to piggyback the chief rather than the other way round. They should never forget that they are on-job trainees for the chief's position.

> *"Deputy has to learn the art of helping the chief while making way for his exit."*

Deputy who becomes chief sees himself as the chief while he was a deputy. The deputy must realize the paucity of time to learn the chief's skills. He should remain coachable and burn the midnight oil. Unless there is a hunger for power, the deputy can't be the chief. He should work for his future and make the chief dependable on him. When the chief starts relaxing deputy begins his journey to the top.

> *"'Willpower' provides the required energy for a deputy to travel the last mile."*

Willpower helps the deputy to focus. Do his homework for the chief's examination. Keeps him coachable. Deputy can be the chief only if he leverages his position to develop acceptance of the team for his elevation. Otherwise, they can be victims of prejudice and pre-judgment. Inorganic growth, the growth by hoping, has certain advantages.

"Deputy's position can be a springboard or a trap."

An intelligent deputy uses his position as a springboard and jumps to the chief's position. The one who refuses to get rid of deputies baggage gets caught in the trap, not knowing how to get out of it. To my surprise, Dick Cheney, one of the most successful politicians in American history, got trapped in the deputy's position. I wonder how such a clever man could not travel that last mile. He remained a rare statesman who remained deputy for both terms to the office. He could not graduate to the President's position. Why? My American readers can add their input on this question.

CHAPTER EIGHTEEN

Succeeding Success- A Leadership Challenge

Great leaders electrify their chairs. Their successor finds it difficult to sit on such an electric chair. They feel the strong current in that chair. We compare the personality of such tall leaders with the new incumbent. Most of the time such comparison is unfair. We compare the character of these great leaders after they achieve success, with the new leaders who are just beginning their tenure. The successor has to manage these expectations which is a great challenge. (Published on Linked on 1 April 2017. Got 100 Likes; 14 Comments and 48 Shares)

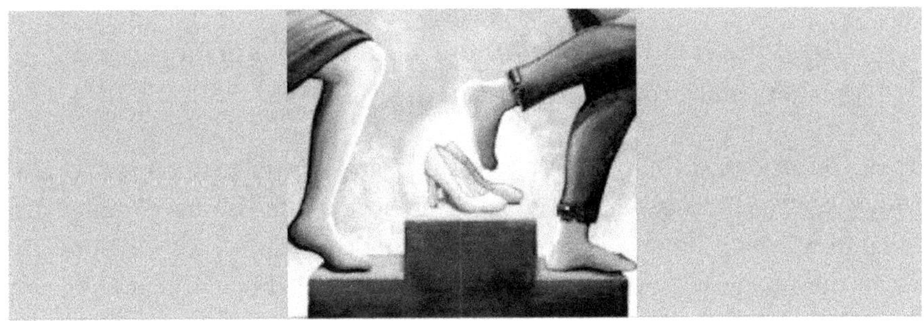

"The successor's dilemma is how to take out the organization from the shadow of the earlier leadership while maintaining the kinetic energy set up by the predecessor."

Imagine becoming captain of the Chicago Bulls basketball team immediately after Michael Jordan or leading Walmart after Sam Walton or Reliance Industries after Dhirubhai Ambani. These could be one of the most difficult things to do. Succeeding after successful leaders can be a real challenge. Tall leaders create leadership brands. They create an aura around their position.

"Some leaders are known because of their powerful chairs; a great leader creates power in his chair."

Great leaders electrify their chairs. Their successor finds it difficult to sit on such an electric chair. They feel the strong current in that chair. We compare the personality of such tall leaders with the new incumbent. Most of the time such comparison is unfair. We compare the character of these great leaders after they achieve success, with the new leaders who are just beginning their tenure. The successor has to manage these expectations which is a great challenge.

From Caterpillar to Butterfly Be it Mahatma Gandhi, Sam Walton, or Nelson Mandela, they had a humble beginning. The experience they went through transformed them into the position for which they are well known.

"Great leaders transform their organizations, but in the process, they get transformed themselves."

They go through the evolution processes from caterpillar to butterfly. The pain & struggle brings them to glory. Their successors also have their share of failures, frustrations, and struggles. Getting compared with the butterfly when they are just a caterpillar is the real pain faced by successors of the great leaders.

"The successor is evaluated by the degree to which he can re-create the outgoing leader's orchestra."

Re-create the orchestra Leaders are like composers who lead an orchestra. Every successful leader creates a band. He is driven by his mission, orchestrating excellent performances. He creates a team of musicians (professionals) who are masters of their instruments (disciplines and departments), perceives a tune (strategy, tactics, and systems), makes everybody play the same tune (teamwork and collective wisdom), and delivers a performance (profits and growth). He inspires the team by giving them the mission. The baton in his hand charges his musicians. _Over the period, his baton becomes a sceptre._

Re-creating that energy is a real tough thing for the successor. Many things are unique to the situation which creates great leaders. A lot of factors contribute to the creation of that situation though the great leader plays a critical role in such a creation. The most important factors could be charged-up employees with a strong sense of purpose and belonging. They put organizational interest before personal interest, work as a team, add value and sacrifice personal interest for the corporate mission. Under such a unique situation, the organization becomes an extended family, and the leader becomes the head of the family. You may think of this as a hypothetical organization, but I have seen at least a couple of such organizations. The first is Indian Oil Corporation which is a Fortune-500 organization. I got associated a few years back as a trainer. I couldn't believe that it was a Govt. undertaking. Their employees were so committed and charged up. Another company which I am following very closely for the last 25 years (since my wife is employed there), is Saraswat Co-operative Bank. It is a Mumbai-based cooperative bank that is doubling its business every 5 to 7 years. When a cooperative sector is in trouble, globally, this bank became Asia's largest cooperative bank, with good profits and very sound business practices. Credit goes to visionary leadership which left behind a legacy, tough to follow. However, the management team groomed by the leadership is maintaining the pace under the new leadership which is equally dynamic.

> "*Re-creating that environment is a real tough thing for the successor. The longer the tenure of the great leader, the larger will be his shadow and more difficult it is to come out of it.*"

The team gets used to his style and starts behaving accordingly. Their behavior becomes a habit and they become impossible to change. Some critical habits become irreversible. I have experienced that when the leader becomes a living legend, the decision-making becomes centralized. Employees happily surrender their powers to the great leader. Many need hand holding. Making decentralization of the decision-making process becomes tough thereafter.

> *"The successor has to struggle with the problem of informal organizations. The aspirants of leadership who remain dormant during the tenure of the great leader form their group and struggle for the crown."*

Other challenges faced by the successor of successful leaders are: Adding value, Maintaining the team, skills, and style, and Maintaining the pace and rhythm.

Adding the value Leadership is not position. It is a responsibility. Leaders are not just auditors they are facilitators. They are navigators. They are change drivers. Successful leaders add a lot of value to their teams.

> *"Leaders are respected on account of their ability to add value in all aspects of management."*

Their contributions may include the ability to attract investors, manage regulators, forecast the business environment, form and hold a motivated team, develop alliances, acquire key accounts, foster innovation, and entrepreneurship, gut-based decision making, etc. Their successors are left with limited options, and they need to be creative in finding out the areas for adding value.

Maintaining the team, skills, and style Many times there are jerks to the team after the change in leadership. A few aspirants for the leadership position become unhappy due to the feeling of rejection. They leave to avoid embarrassment. While leaving they take a few good employees with them and create a skill vacuum in the organization. They break the scalar chain of the organization. Some good employees with unique skills might leave due to the fear of a change in the management style. New leadership and the circle around it might create a fear psychosis. Employees who are not friendly with them, due to historical reasons, become their victims.

Maintaining the pace and rhythm Great leaders set organizations in a rhythm and set the pace for business development and organizational growth. The successor has to maintain the pace and rhythm.

"Wise successors try to maintain the status quo after taking over the position rather than trying to implement radical reforms in a great hurry."

They avoid any premeditated actions and rather wait for their turn and the right opportunity. They use this pause to organize their strategy and refine their tactics. They trigger the action only after ensuring the stability of the team, pace, and rhythm. They remain unperturbed by the early criticism and evaluation of their work. The successor exercises his right to use a different leadership style rather than just bench-marking his predecessor. Progressive countries like USA, UK, China & India have seen successful leaders one after another but have different leadership styles. Business organizations that became industry leaders also benefited from various leaders having different leadership styles.

"As long as the 'Mission' remains the same different leaders can have different styles."

Leadership styles are like methods in mathematics. The same problem (mission) can be solved by different methods (leadership styles). Some methods can be shorter but difficult to understand while others can be easy but time-consuming. The superiority of the method depends on the situation. For competitive exams with pressure on time, shorter methods are useful and for university exams detailing all the steps and the formula is important. Similarly, leadership styles are a function of situations.

"Under different situations different leadership styles become successful."

That is the reason people debate whether Mahatma Gandhi's leadership style would have delivered results in the case of Hitler or Stalin ruling India in the place of the British. Whether today's generation will accept him as the leader of the nation? Could Mao raise to power in China, in the 21st century?

Smart successors understand the DNA of their organization. They wait for their turn, Take baby steps, initially, while triggering a change. Stick to their own leadership style rather than copying the earlier leader's style. They understand the situation is specific to their organization well and then choose their leadership style accordingly. They focus on the mission and ensure that the pace and motto developed during the earlier leader don't get disturbed. They understand the myths and hype which surround successful leaders. They try to put organizational image before the leader's image. Such successors succeed. They take the organization higher by making it stronger. Such succession is the mark of a great organization. Sam Walton formed Walmart and made it the number one retailer in America. His successors who were groomed by Sam himself took Walmart to a higher level. In 1992 when Sam passed away Walmart was around $50 billion. Today it is nearing $ 500 billion. Ten-fold growth in 25 years. Sam's successors made Walmart not just the largest retailer in the world but the largest company in the world ranked #1 on the Fortune -500 list.

"The successor's success also goes to the earlier leader. He gets credited for choosing, grooming, and creating the culture and support systems. "

This explains the success of Korean Chaebols and other successful family-managed businesses in India.

CHAPTER NINETEEN

Leadership – A Skyscraper TightRope Walk

eadership is like walking on a tight rope hung between two towers that are 110 floors high. The Hollywood movie, 'The walk' highlights the qualities of leadership required in order to achieve any mega success, be it personal or organizational. (It was published on LinkedIn on 1 April 2017. Got 63 Likes, 3 Comments, and 41 Shares).

Recently I saw a Hollywood movie, 'The Walk', in my home theatre. I bought a 3D Blu-Ray from America during my last trip, in Oct 2016. It is a 1974 true story about a Frenchman, Philippe Petite. He stretched a rope between the twin towers of the World Trade Centre, in Manhattan New York, illegally, and walked back and forth on it. The rope was tied about 1350 feet above the ground level. He not just walked on the rope at that height but sat, slept, and even danced on it. Most importantly, he did not use any hook or a safety net. It was his crazy mission for which he prepared himself, formed a team, inspired it, and practiced hard for over six and half years. Watch the trailer for the movie on Youtube.

Leader - A Man on Wire While I was watching the movie carefully I suddenly found a leader in action. Is the leadership about walking the tightrope on top of the skyscrapers? Just look at the life on this tightrope, is it not similar to the life of a leader? The fear of vertigo, chasing the mission, the ability to garner support, the amount of risk, rewards of success everything is similar. Leader chases a seemingly impossible mission, Not to prove supremacy but to achieve a sense of fulfillment. The goals set by him are so high that they might trigger vertigo. They take a risk in scaling the height.

"Leaders are magnets that pull people around them, naturally."

'Privacy' may be the only thing that leaders hardly get. They are 'people persons'. His challenge is not attracting people but otherwise. His people are possessive of him and demand an unfair share of his time. Managing this emotional need and demand on his time is a challenge. Successful leaders get recognition & rewards for themselves and for their team. Philippe shared many qualities with admired leaders. Just look at him as a clone of the respected leaders. You will find many analogies.

Driven by Passion and Mission Philippe was so passionate about the tightrope walking that he didn't hesitate to throw his life at it. Leaders are also very passionate. Most of us have our passions, but we hardly do anything about it. We just keep dreaming about it. Some feel that passion is personal and one should not invest professional time in it. We keep promising ourselves that we would follow our passion 'someday'. As we start climbing the career steps, we keep re-scheduling our plan to follow our passion. Finally, we realize that we are too busy to follow our passion and resolve to devote time once we take retirement.

"Admired leaders turn their passion into the profession."

The birth of the leader Lucky person finds his passion in the early period of his life. After some time they find it impossible to manage their passion and profession separately. When thrown to the wall they dare to follow their passion. They start living for their passion. They put their potential energy and kinetic energy into their passion. In due course of time, they create a blast mesmerizing people. This dazzling impact attracts people around them who start following them. The star is born. The leader is born. Leaders find their mission in their passion. Passion drives mission. Emotions drive humans. They provide the impetus. Emotion is a bio-fuel. Passion is an intense and uncontrollable emotion. It is an atomic fuel. The mission needs to be fueled by passion. A deeper passion is required for the mission impossible.

"Passion is the mark of the 'man on a mission.'"

Sets Crazy Mission and Hit it Hard When Philippe set his mind on the venture of walking the tightrope between the twin towers, people thought he was crazy. The Leader's crazy idea becomes his identity. Passionate people get dreams which get crystallized in the form of a mission. When he shares it with like-minded people, they accept it and swear by it. Such a man on a mission becomes the leader and gathers the organization around him. He also sells his idea to other team members.

"The leader's mission becomes an organizational mission. Some acquire it organically others are sold on it by the leader."

Other people see the leader's mission as a crazy venture till the time it becomes a reality. After Philippe had completed his skyscraper walk successfully, NYPD (New York Police Department) arrested him for the illegal walk. He became a national hero only when the news of his arrest gets broken in the media.

Do not Dilute the Mission Philippe was advised to use a hook or the safety net to prevent any eventuality. But he firmly refused the proposal. He thought it would weaken him and undermine his achievement. He didn't settle for the less. He didn't use a hook. Great leaders do not find short-cuts. They know there are no elevators to success, one has to take the staircase. They are not obsessed with recognition. They are driven by a sense of achievement. Recognition is the confirmation by the external world. The sense of achievement is self-realization. It is internal. The diluting of a mission brings guilt. Sticking to it brings pride.

> *"Great leaders are worried more about their self-image rather than their public image. They are at peace when their public image matches their self-image. Conscience is their mirror where they check their self-image."*

Leaders are Fearless Philippe had earlier broken his ribs when he fell from the rope, in a Paris show. But he did not fear the height of the world trade center, the twin towers. They were the tallest towers in the world though. He was so excited by the idea to walk the tightrope between the twin towers that he had no time to think about the possibility of failure. It was not even an option for him. Great Leaders are drawn their power from their sense of purpose. They overcome their fears.

> *"The leader's fear gets dissolved in self-belief and lust for the mission."*

Philippe's walk on the wire was illegal and NYPD booked him for the offense. (All charges were dismissed in exchange for him doing a performance in Central Park for children.) Court of the New York state later termed it the 'artistic crime of the century'. But the violation of law and the punishment after that was a non-factor for Philippe.

> *"The foundation of fearlessness is the confidence leaders draw from the nobility of intentions, collective expertise, discipline, faith and practice."*

Leaders make their team and charge them with a sense of purpose Philippe knew what he could do on his own and where he would need support from his team.

Leaders are team players. They identify the needs of the organization and spot the talent to satisfy them. They understand the difficulty in retaining the talent and making it work for the mission. Many times the acquired talent may not have the same mission. Leaders have a great skill to imbibe the mission on the talent. Philippe's mission was sold to his team by him.

Leaders are the best salespersons who sell internally. They sell the mission and the approach required to be adopted for fulfilling the mission.

Leaders have the power of delegation Philippe knew an expert tightrope walker who was extraordinary in tying tight ropes. He takes significant efforts to convince him on providing the knowledge on the type of rope and kind of knots required. Leaders develop a sense of delegation. They know exactly what to delegate, whom to delegate, how much to delegate, how to follow up, etc.

Practice " Don't practice until you get it right. Practice until you can't get it wrong!" This was the principle that was observed by Philippe while following his passion. Leaders practice so hard that they take out the third dimension of their difficulty, making it just a two-dimensional plane that is easy to tackle.

Discipline is the most divine thing for the leader. Be it a time or behavior or spending resources leaders are very disciplined. They are least tolerant when it comes to the following discipline. Leaders do not negotiate the implementation of the discipline. They practice what they preach when it comes to discipline.

> *"The discipline is sancrosanct. It can't be treded-off for performanace. Even the top performers have to follow the discipline. Rather it is more important for them."*

When I was working for the Piramal Group of Companies, I always saw our Chairman Ajay Piramal, the billionaire, walking into the venue of the annual sales conference at least ten minutes before the inaugural time. He never used morning traffic jams in Mumbai as an excuse for getting late. He always factored in that variable. Traffic jams only determined how many minutes before the time would he reach the conference venue. Discipline is the critical value of the leader.

Leaders seek advice from masters Leaders respect masters. They identify champions in the required fields who have the required knowledge and seek their advice. Philippe took the advice of many masters. A German juggler financed his project by giving him valuable advice. He sought advice on the kind of rope and other tools to be used during the show.

Leaders develop unique tools and techniques Leaders have out-of-box ideas on tools and techniques. When faced with an acute shortage of water, Reliance used seawater for cooling in the refinery. Bruce Lee invented many tools and techniques of defense.

In a nutshell, Philippe, his mission, team, and the situation mirror leadership. Aspiring leaders must watch the movie and learn their lessons.

CHAPTER TWENTY

Alert and Alive Leadership

Businesses are facing a macro-environment that is highly fluid requiring dynamic strategic planning. The leadership has to be alert and alive. Their reactions should be like reflexes, quick & accurate. Competitors can catch you on the wrong foot if they find you napping. The long-term plan is becoming more of a hurdle than a tool that enables growth. Gone are the days when the governments used to prepare a five-year plan and swear by it. Even the Government of India has abolished the planning commission. Leaders are looking for flexibility in planning. In fact, the alert and alive customers demand alive brands and alert marketers. (Published on LinkedIn on 21 August 2018. Got 201 Likes; 24 Comments and 15 Shares)

Who could imagine that one of the most successful supermarket companies in America, 'Whole Foods' would be on sale? Amazon bought it for USD 13.7 billion. Facebook buying 'WhatsApp' was equally shocking. Their competitors had to alter their strategic plans to accommodate this development. An electrified business environment gives high voltage shocks which can be fatal. Business leaders can't afford to go off-line or 'out of range'. Modern-day leaders have to be 'hands-on'. They stay close to customers. So close that they can smell the behavioral changes and listen to the customer murmur, any private expression of discontent. They can en-cash the demographic dividends instantly. Alert and alive leaders can recover from dropping market share swiftly.

> *"In today's business environment staying ahead requires out-foxing, out-pacing, and over-powering the competitors."*

A deer can run at a speed of 80 km per hour. It can jump 10 feet high and 30 feet long. A cheetah has to be really alert and alive. His task is two-fold, to run faster than the deer and also to grab it. Cheetahs can run at 90 to 110 kms per hour. Once they spot the prey they hardly lose it. In this race of life and death, the one who is alert and alive wins the race for survival. In fact, only that deer, out of the herd, which is not alert and alive becomes the prey. Market leaders and challengers have to match the competencies of Cheetah. They have to run fast but they can't trade off agility for speed. Their ability to change direction swiftly while chasing competitors at a great pace will define their success. Alert and alive leaders can spot the changes quickly and jump for the opportunities, even threats can be fend-off successfully.

Innovation creates disruption: Innovative companies are the real threat in the market. They trigger disruptions through their innovations. Apple launched iPhone in mid-2007 and changed the concept of the mobile phone to pocket computers. Just within 7 years, in the year 2014, Apple rose to the market leader's position.

> *"Disruption damages the market leaders who are not alert and alive."*

Nokia, the market leader, zeroed down on developing quality mobile phones with superb sound quality. They were too busy doing it. They missed an important development, smartphones, which disrupted the mobile market. Nokia was busy developing mobile for video conferencing and location detecting. The lack of alertness cost Nokia the market leadership and they had to sell their business to Microsoft for $ 7.2 billion. This disruption, which wiped out the global leader, happened just in 5 years (in the year 2011).

"Leaders have to develop an organizational culture of being alert and alive."

The top leadership of Nokia realized that the change was coming but the middle-level management was over-confident and assumed that their technical competencies were impossible to match. They were not alert and alive. While Nokia was boasting their core competency of manufacturing quality phones, their technology was made obsolete by the competitors, making the quality and reliability redundant.

"Companies can't sleep on their past laurels. They have to remain alert and alive always."

In India, Nokia had more than 22% market share of mobile telephones in 2012. It came down to 9% in just one year. Samsung caught Nokia napping. In 2014, Samsung acquired a 30% market share but Samsung didn't remain alert and alive either. Xiaomi pushed Samsung to the number two position in 2017, within just 3 years from Xiaomi's launch in the Indian market. Samsung could hold on to the leadership position only for 5 years. They didn't remain alert and alive to the entry of Chinese mobile brands into the Indian market. Chinese brands appealed to the Indian masses due to their 'value for money' approach while Samsung was busy in up-selling.

"The market share is no longer an entry barrier. Bigger the market leader, the more alert and alive it needs to be."

Bajaj Auto had been the market leader in the Indian scooter industry for over two decades. Honda, with its 'Activa' model, wiped out Bajaj within three years of the launch of Activa in the Indian scooter market. Activa, did up-selling, while Bajaj wanted to sell cheaper scooters that were obsolete. Bajaj did not remain alert and alive to the changing customer preferences and failed to adapt to modern technologies like auto-gear and button-start. Bajaj discontinued the scooter model assuming that it was in the decline stage of the product life cycle. The alert and alive Honda rejuvenated the product life cycle, snatching the market leadership. After one and half decades Bajaj is rethinking and planning to relaunch the scooter. In the car industry the highest market share by any leader in any country, other than India, is 17.5%. Maruti-Suzuki is alert and alive even after grabbing the leadership position. It enjoys about 50% market share in the Indian car industry. Maruti-Suzuki is being chased by seven Global Fortune-500 car companies but together they hold a market share less than that of Maruti-Suzuki. Power comes to Maruti-Suzuki because they are alert and alive. They are unassuming, vigilant, and reactive. They hardly ignore any development in the market.

"Companies like Maruti-Suzuki, Walmart, and ICICI bank are hungry. Their greed for growth keeps them on their toes."

ICICI bank in India is another example of alert and alive leadership. In terms of the number of assets managed they are the second largest bank in India. ICICI bank has about 3540 branches, 11200 ATMs, and over 82000 employees. The bank manages assets worth 100 billion USD. In the banking industry, they are known for their hunger for growth. Their performance culture puts a lot of pressure on employees but they are always alert and alive. It helped them become the second largest bank in India where the banking sector is highly regulated. They achieved this distinction in just two decades. Samsonite is my favorite brand. As you can see in the adjoining graph, Samsonite controls the global market share more than the top 9 players put together. They are always alert and alive through their innovations. Their designs, materials, and workmanship keep them ahead of the competition. While most luggage brands have been struggling to maintain quality and reliability, Samsonite offers luggage that lasts for years and looks fresh always. Now they are developing a smart suitcase which will be fitted with a microchip. It will help to find the lost bag through GPS. Why were horses used in battles? They are always at work. They sleep less than 3 hours a day. They sleep anytime during the day. Most of their sleep is in the standing position, often with open eyes. Probably, they are the most alert and alive animals found useful to humans. Great leaders are like horses. They get charged up after short sleep. They are always alert and keep their team alive.

"India is being developed by those who work over weekends."

Great leaders from developing countries know the value of working harder and for extended hours. They promote working on Saturdays. They believe that working a day extra every week is the best way to catch up with the developed world. It helps in remaining alert and alive when the Western competitors are napping.

n a nutshell, the secret to the success of great companies, brands, and leaders is staying alert and alive. It is their core competency that helps them as a competitive tool. By staying alert they can spot the opportunity or threat much before their competitors and they can be alive to such developments. Staying alert and alive helps not only the challengers and followers but is required for the market leader as well.

CHAPTER TWENTY-ONE

Alignment : The Art of Agreement

Migrating birds have developed a technique to fly with less energy so they can fly hundreds of miles. This technic is alignment. Leaders can train their teams to get aligned. This can save organizational resources which are wasted in overcoming internal resistance. Alignment can bring synergy and optimize organizational resources. Alignment gets the organization to cruise in auto mode. (Published on LinkedIn on 14 October 2018. Got 39 Likes; 29 Comments and 31 Shares).

If two people agree on everything then one of them is not required. If they don't agree on anything both are not required.

Humans think differently by the design. Their preferences, likes, dislikes, and tastes are always different. Alignment is not about giving up differences. It is about retaining the identity, maintaining the differences but still getting integrated to create the synergistic effect.

> *"Alignment is not mixing and losing identity. It is about remaining different and adding the value of contrast."*

Alignment is not about creating friction with other personalities but about creating an aesthetic value by remaining in contrast. Alignment doesn't create aberrations and heat or friction, it generates a pleasant fragrance. It makes the team feel that they are taking a stroll in a garden with beautiful trees in different colors. flowers and fragrances. Alignment is like getting arranged in a bouquet. Every member of the team maintains his unique color but enhances the total impact by joining other beautiful but distinctly different flowers. Any good organization is such a bouquet of unique personalities who are different than each other but together generate a much larger impact. Alignment is always for a purpose. People can be distinctly different otherwise but when they come together for a purpose they align. The alignment is with the cause rather than with the people. How we maintain unity in diversity determines the success of our organization.

> *"Alignment doesn't aim at cutting down on variety. It is standing out in formation."*

The rationale for Alignment There is a strong logic behind alignment. It is a formation that generates energy. It is the formation (structure) of diversity. It weaves divergent views, styles, personalities, and other components of the organization together. It pushes other members of the team. Alignment places every team member in a unique position in such a way that he contributes maximum energy to the cause. The team creates a pool of energy and helps everybody to perform to their potential.

"Alignment formulates a molecule with the mission as a nucleus and organizational resources as electrons revolving around it."

The formation of a flock influences aerodynamics. As the birds flap their wings, the air flowing off their wing tips gives birds in the back an extra lift. The amount of energy the birds need to fly is reduced, by this lift, making it easier for the birds to fly. Stronger birds fly ahead of others because it is difficult to maintain the energy level in the front. However, they maintain rotation to provide exposure to younger members and also to rest the seniors.

Role of a Leader A leader plays important role in the alignment of his team. He makes his team members realize their unique strengths and also challenges. He shows them the path of alignment. The leader convinces his team that the only way to manage their challenges is by aligning with team members who are strong in those areas. The leader makes the team understand the value of being different than others. In their formation, they blend the benefits of experience and youth. They keep the positions rotating to avoid fatigue failure & also to develop the younger talent.

"Great leaders nurture diversity and they have the ability to align the diversity."

America and Japan Why is America progressing year after year? Why is Japan going down year by year? The root cause is diversity. American leaders have nurtured diversity. They have attracted technology talent from India, Korea, and China but also admitted hardworking Latinos. Great American leaders have nicely aligned talent with hard work. Japanese blocked immigration. They were obsessed with maintaining their 'purity'. They saw immigrants as invaders of their culture. Their inability to nurture diversity is making them lose in the race for economic supremacy.

"Aligning is not following blindly. It is a conscious and cautious effort to reduce the gap and friction while en-cashing the dividend of diversity."

Aligning the Structure (teamwork) Structure plays a critical role in organizational success. McKinsey's Seven 'S' model of organizational effectiveness identifies a structure as important hardware for global dominance. The structure is the alignment of manpower which is the most valuable resource of the organization. The structure is hardware whereas alignment is software. Structure can't be successful unless team members align themselves.

> *"Alignment in the structure is required in terms of 'shared values' and 'collective wisdom'."*

Shared values are the binder that binds the team together. The leader has to really struggle very hard to establish shared values and develop collective wisdom. The higher the diversity, the more difficult will be to establish shared values and collective wisdom. Diversity brings cultural differences. They are difficult to integrate. Great leaders focus on developing a tolerance for different cultures and aligning all sub-cultures to create a unique organizational culture. The collective wisdom of an organization gets reflected in organizational policies and processes. For organizational success, it is important that team members should align themselves with the policies and processes. In the management cliche, it is called 'compliance' and 'Due diligence.

> *"Alignment goes beyond compliance and due diligence. It focuses the minds, hearts, and brains of the team members on the mission."*

The team members take 'the initiative' and try to innovate different business processes. The personal interests of the members of the team become subordinate to the interests of the organization. The primary focus is maintained on the organizational objectives rather than on the objectives of the individual team members.

> *"Henry Fayol's Principles of Management indicate the need for alignment"*

Alignment and Principles of Management Most of the principles of management identified by Henry Fayol revolve around alignment. An alignment requires 'Unity of Direction' and 'Unity of command' and also the 'Discipline' to maintain them. 'Division of work' requires establishing a clear 'Authority and responsibility' relationship and also the 'scalar chain' to ensure continuity. They together form the basis for alignment. The leader has to strike balance between 'the degree of centralization and delegation. Setting them in the right proportion is alignment. 'Order', 'Equity', 'Initiative', and 'Stability of tenure' form the eco-system of alignment. Together these principles build alignment and ensure 'Espirit De Corps'.

> *"Alignment brings focus and a great leader maintains this focus on the mission."*

Internal and External Alignment The real challenge to the leadership is maintaining internal and external alignment. Employees need to align to the mission. They are required to align with the team. They also need alignment with shared values and collective wisdom. The same things are required to be maintained externally. The collaborators like suppliers, Wholesalers, and retailers have to be aligned with the organizational philosophy, business model, collective wisdom, systems and processes, and employees. The external validity of the alignment is much more difficult but it is critical to provide a unique customer experience.

> *"Alignment with a mission, customer delight, nature (Sustainability), and commercial realities differentiates successful organizations from the rest."*

Mission and customers are the purposes of any business. Customers are to be served to achieve the organizational mission. A mission becomes impossible if it harms commercial viability and nature. Great leaders keep a perfect balance between customer delight and commercial viability. They achieve it by aligning the organization and its ecosystem with social responsibility and sustainability.

Gut Feel – The Leader's Compass

Leaders have a better gut feeling management. Many leaders first develop gut and then search for the evidence, before making decisions. Leaders have the courage to follow their gut feeling. They know the risk involved with gut-based decision-making, but still, they dare it. Sometimes they are compelled to take the risk due to their role in the team. (Published on LinkedIn on 22 March 2017. Got 810 Likes; and also 28 Comments; 175 Shares).

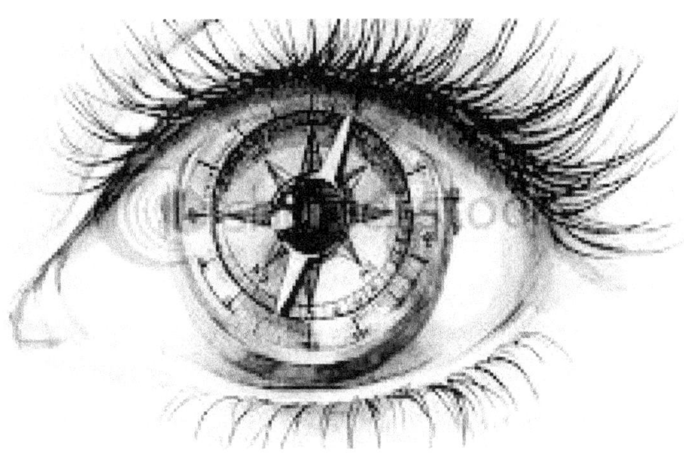

The world leader comes from the word 'to lead' which means showing the path. The leader is somebody who shows the way. Leaders have a strong sense of direction. They also have an organ that others do not have, a biological compass. They know very well which direction lies the opportunity and where is the threat. While leaders listen carefully to people and assess many advisers on the possible orientations, they tend to follow their inner voice.

> **"A leader's Conviction is the most important intangible asset of the organization."**

Google is working very hard on its self-driving car project, Waymo. But still, Waymo could not replace the human factor entirely. Similarly, management has developed many scientific methods, tools, models, and processes to get in the right direction. But they could not replace the human element, the leader's gut feeling, in the decision-making. The 'management compass' is developed by collective efforts over a few decades. The management compass which directs businesses is the product of rational thinking, research, and experiences. The most traditional method of decision-making is an iterative process. In this process, the alternatives are developed and they are tested for optimality. The process starts with the first option and continues till the choice with optimal value is discovered. It is identified as rational decision-making that is sensible.

Many leaders respect the scientific decision-making processes, but they may not follow them, at all incidences. Surprisingly, on many occasions

> **"The leader's biological compass overpowers the scientific management compass, particularly in an unstructured, chaotic environment."**

The leader could beeline to his task due to his intuition. It is the way by which their brain helps them to decide. Intuition may be defined as understanding something without any conscious recourse to thought, observation, or reason. Every human has a gut feeling. We sense something without knowing why. But leaders have better gut feeling management.

Many leaders first develop gut and then search for the evidence, before making decisions. Leaders have the courage to follow their gut feeling. They know the risk involved with gut-based decision-making, but still, they dare it. Sometimes they are compelled to take the risk due to their role in the team. We try to avoid or reduce the risk.

"Leaders try to reduce the impact of the risk rather than avoid it. They develop a recovery plan for the unfavorable outcome."

That is how leaders are different from the rest of us.

Why do leaders have a stronger gut feeling? Leaders are placed higher in structure hence they have a better perspective. They can see things which we can't because of the height. They have a broader canvas and get to know the whole picture. We see things in parts. We get bogged down by contemporary issues; leaders are futuristic. They interact with many people from different backgrounds and disciplines hence they get to know the flip side of the decision better. Leaders are optimistic. They have to provide hope to others even in a hopeless situation. Providing hope needs optimism which leads to certain risk-taking.

How do leaders develop gut feelings? It is a black box. Nobody knows how to draw up the gut feeling systematically. But there is evidence that it grows through exposure, experience, practice, training, etc.

"Grooming may be the best method to develop gut feelings."

Grooming requires careful selection of the candidate. It can be done with only a few candidates, mostly one. The mentor who will be grooming the candidate must be the leader himself. Grooming is done with the objective of succession planning. The result of grooming is that the candidate replaces the mentor in the organizational hierarchy. While grooming, the mentor provides opportunities for the candidate to make decisions in unstructured situations, in chaotic situations. Such exposure helps in the development of gut-based decision-making.

"Grooming is developing leaders, on the job. The candidates feel the heat, pressure, and friction which forge the gut feel."

Grooming is learning by hand holding. Only lucky people get to learn by this method. The quality of the experience depends on the quality of the boss. Working with leaders offers out-of-world experience. Grooming is a very tough experience mentally and physically but worth it because of the opportunity in the future to get into the leader's shoes and the chance to be trained by the leader himself. It helps in developing a biological compass.

Adversities contribute to developing a gut feeling. Adversities teach you how and when things can go wrong. They provide insight into failure and negative energy. Adversities also develop your confidence to face them better when they re-occur. Working in a particular organization for a longer duration provides you with the exposure and experiences of the boom and also the recession.

Why do Indian leaders take gut-based decisions? Developed economies have stable macro-environment, and set systems and processes. In developing countries like India, the leaders have to deal with the unstructured and chaotic environment. Additionally, they struggle with the resource crunch. Most of the problems are non-routine in nature and the inadequacy of the data makes it difficult to use analytics in the decision-making like their western counterparts. Heterogeneity of the team members regarding education, culture, and experience makes it difficult to adopt 'consensus-based decision-making' which is common in German and Japanese management. Having ruled out the other decision-making systems like decision-making using analytics and consensus-based decision-making, Indian leaders are forced to resort to gut-based decision-making.

In a nutshell gut-based, decisions making can't be replaced in totality although the gut can be made stronger by resorting to other methods such as supplements.

Leveraging – A Core Leadership Skill

Leveraging is using a lever, which is a type of tool, to reduce the efforts required to lift a load. It is easier to lift the heavier object using a lever rather than trying to lift it directly. In simple words leveraging is getting much more as an output compared to the input. This happens due to some factors or tools. Identifying such factors and devising such tools, to gain higher output, is the leveraging skill. Leadership has to identify the strengths/advantages of their organization, scale them up and leverage them to gain industry leadership. (Published on LinkedIn on 26 June 2017. Had 40 Likes; 2 Comments and 1 Share).

"Leveraging is scaling up an advantage. Great leaders spot an advantage and magnify it to get leverage."

They know which advantages can be leveraged and which can't. They can have the ability to scale up the advantage. Some country leaders leverage their natural resources like skilled/unskilled manpower, geography, etc to achieve economic progress. Dutch leadership leveraged strategic location to develop their port, Rotterdam, as a logistic hub in Europe. They constructed a canal, Nieuwe Waterweg, which opened in 1872 and has a length of approximately 20.5 kilometers. The advantage was further scaled-up by constructing state of an art highway and railway system which connected Rotterdam to the entire Europe. The result was visible. European importers and exporters prefer to route their consignments through Rotterdam rather than the ports in their own countries because it was faster, cheaper, and more convenient. Until 2004, Rotterdam was the largest port in the world until another visionary leader, Kuan Lee of Singapore, saw the advantage that the global production center was moving towards the far eastern countries like China, and Malaysia from Europe. He developed Singapore port by scaling up the advantage of the geographic vicinity and dislodged Rotterdam from the number one position. Visionary leadership in Italy developed product design skills in cars and luxury products. Japan scaled up its talent in consumer electronics.

"Indian and Chinese leadership have not yet leveraged agriculture because of their inability to scale up the advantages."

Their advantages are fertile land, fixed and good rains during a specific period, and the knowledge of agriculture. Can be magnified by: getting into food processing/preservation and creating a global distribution system that they will control. Possible result: dominance in the world food supply.

Leveraging An Adversity Great leaders demonstrated how even adversity can be fought by leveraging it as a blessing in disguise. Bangladesh leveraged its poverty by offering skilled, trained, and cheap textile labor to become the second largest garment exporter in the world. Israel leveraged water scarcity to develop drip and sprinkler irrigation systems and also other modern agricultural tools and techniques. This country is on barren land but teaches agriculture to traditionally farming countries.

"Leadership defines whether to be the beneficiary or the victim of adversity."

Countries like Afghanistan, Palestine, and Iraq couldn't become the production centers of the world, like Bangladesh because their leaders couldn't convert adversity to advantage and magnify it to gain leverage. They continue to be victims of adversity. It can be a very effective technic to fight with limited resources. It can multiply productivity & profits multi-fold. The leveraging can be done absolutely by anything.

"A so-called disadvantage can be leveraged to gain a competitive advantage."

The core of Kung Fu is power, agility, stamina, and most importantly ability to leverage. Kung Fu teaches how to leverage domestic articles or any other item & use it as a weapon, in the case of a sudden attack. It teaches how to leverage your weight, height, and most of the body senses. It doesn't treat short people at disadvantage. You may be tall or short, hefty or thin, ready with a weapon or without it, you can always defend yourself in the case of an attack by leveraging anything you have or anything around you which has some advantage. Leveraging has many uses even in management and leadership. Financial leveraging means making investments of a much higher amount than just the owner's funds and thus increasing the overall return. Owners' funds are leveraged to collect required finances in terms of loans. Generally, the higher, the leverage better the financial management, though the risk in ownership of the assets also goes up. If the rate of return is higher than the interest rate then financial leveraging works to your advantage.

Leveraging to create wealth Industry leaders like Bill Gates and Warren Buffet became the richest men in the world, not due to the accumulated operational profits but due to leveraging their capital. They invested in the companies they owned. They became rich because their companies became successful and the share price shot up. The demand for their company shares increased the share price hence they became rich.

"Branding concepts like umbrella branding, brand extensions, brand endorsement, etc are nothing but leveraging goodwill. Brand extensions leverage the consumer franchise which is already created in a particular product category to a different product category."

Moral of the story. Leadership has to identify the strengths/advantages of their organization, scale them up and leverage them to gain industry leadership. If you face adversity, don't worry, think about how can you leverage it. Leaders can survive and thrive if they develop the art, talent, and skill of leveraging

Managing Access : Lessons from History

Most leaders are busy people. Time is the most scarce resource for them. They can't spare time for everybody who demands their time. They have to be choosy. Access to the leader is a privilege. I have seen many people making their careers out of such access. Some use it responsibly, some use it sparingly but most of them overuse it and even misuse it. This article is about managing such privileged access to power. If not handled properly, access can even ruin the leadership. Human history offers many examples and modern-day management leaders must draw their lessons from those stories. (Published on LinkedIn on- 11 November 2017. Got 184 Likes; 39 Comments and 39 Shares).

Historically in Greece, the Middle East, China, Korea, and other parts of the far east countries eunuchs played an important role during different dynasties. Castration was typically carried out on the soon-to-be eunuch without his consent in order that he might perform a specific social function. The earliest records for such intentional castration to produce eunuchs are from the Sumerian city, Lagash (presently in Iraq) in the 21st century BC. Read here (https://en.wikipedia.org/wiki/Eunuch). Eunuchs performed a wide variety of functions in many different cultures: courtiers or equivalent domestics, royal guards, govt. officials, and guardians of women. They were reliable servants of royal courts where physical access to a ruler could wield great influence. They performed low domestic works like cutting the hair of the king, preparing his bed, bathing him etc. Eunuchs had an access to the 'king's ear' which imparted the 'de facto' power to them. In China, the tradition of using eunuchs in the imperial court goes back at least 2,000 years. During the Han Dynasty (206 B.C." A.D. 220), palace eunuchs often ran the day to day affairs of the court. They vied for power with military leaders, scholar & bureaucrats.

"Beginning with the reign of Han Shun To in A.D. 126, eunuchs held a high position in the Chinese court and had what is known today as access."

While ministers and many high officials were not allowed to address the Emperor directly, eunuchs saw him on a daily basis and were allowed to talk to him on familiar terms. In China, eunuchs became so powerful that they became an object of envy. The scholars & bureaucrats, who had risen to their positions through merit, "feared, envied and despised" the eunuchs. Soon eunuchs realized the fact that their access to the 'kings ear' was a bigger asset than the positions held by bureaucrats or the respect commanded by scholars. This realization made them greedy, corrupt and scheming. They started corrupt and immoral practices. They started selling the access. They often demanded kickbacks in return for contracts. Any senior official with a business that demanded the emperor's attention had to persuade a eunuch to carry the message for him; the eunuchs, naturally enough, asked for fees in return for such services, the more powerful ones were bribed and flattered by ambitious officials. Does this ring a bell? Haven't you seen enough of them in the modern day offices? Are they not controlling the bosses? Are they not closer to his ears than most of you are?

In the good old days, few persons would happily get castrated in order to be near to the power. Can you not see the similar behavior today?

"The ultra-modern 'corporate eunuchs' cut-off their important organ, self-esteem, in order to stay near to power."

They project themselves as lions. They may or may not know their worth but they desperately want to prove their worth. They have limited ability to contribute hence they leverage their access to the leadership. Weak members of the team depend on them as their advocate. They are prepared to 'compensate' for the favors done to them. Such people create informal organizations within the organizations. It is called the cartel or the 'pressure lobby'.

"Stronger the leader stronger will be the corporate eunuch."

Why are the corporate eunuchs dangerous? In the history, eunuchs were either born or forced to be eunuchs. But these modern-day 'corporate eunuchs' do it willfully. They are more dangerous. Their insecure mind is the source of their jealousy towards talented performers. They are a source of discontentment in the organizations. They are the parasites who flourish on corruption.

"Corporate eunuchs realize that the access to power is the greatest nuisance power which can be encashed."

They frustrate the performers. Corporate eunuchs have no concern about the organizational mission or vision. Their mission is to propagate their vested agenda. Their loyalty to the leader is also not beyond doubt. They could leave the leader in a crisis like mice in a sinking ship. How should the leaders deal with it? Leaders should have a secured mind themselves. My experience is that most of the times leaders themselves are the source of this problem. Eunuchs are creations of the insecure leaders.

"Insecure leaders create corporate eunuchs."

Some leaders like sycophancy. They always want to be in a company of people who praise them. Such leaders are not open to evaluation by others. They evaluate themselves. This evaluation is not objective and it has no negative marks. But they need endorsements by others. They want only sounding boards & not genuine advisors who are fearless & provide their views without any vested interest.

Sycophants are potential corporate eunuchs.

Some leaders are not self-reliant. They are over-dependent on others for secretarial assistance and for many things. If you are not driving your car yourself then you are inviting a potential corporate eunuch who can follow your actions and reactions because he is your driver. Initially, he drives your car as per your directions after a few years he starts giving you directions and drives you crazy and arrives at his destination.

"Do-It-Yourself (DIY) culture reduces the possibilities of the birth of corporate eunuchs."

Secretarial assistance should be replaced by technology. The leaders have to be techno-savvy & should use modern-day gadgets, apps, and other tools like "Siri' on iPhone, google calendar, google maps, GPS, etc along with social media like Linked In, and Facebook, Whatsapp, etc. Another way is to remain accessible. The leader should create enough listening posts and avoid staying in the 'forbidden city'. Creating multiple access channels reduces the power of corporate eunuchs. How to deal with organizational eunuchs? The best method is to establish active communication with the leaders. Sharing the work progress, promptly with the leader would help. In rural India, people say that 'the dog which walks beneath the bullock cart pretends that the bullock cart moves because of him.' Corporate eunuchs are like these dogs who undermine the efforts of a bullock. They make their living by undermining the efforts of loyal and hardworking employees. The best policy could be remaining neutral and not joining any cartel as it may give you benefits in the short term but will definitely harm you in the long term. Please remember

"The corporate eunuchs are friends to nobody"

Trees live for hundreds of years but parasites have short lives. They thrive during spring and vanish in fall. But they can kill a weak tree. Follow the tree, don't follow the parasites.

CHAPTER TWENTY-FIVE

Managing Glamour: A Leadership Challenge

Political and corporate leaders are blessed with glamour. Their greatness lies in their ability to provide energy from their aura to their team. The glittering aura lightens up their journey toward their mission. Glamorous leaders are required to take initiative in making collaborative efforts. Handling glamour determines the taste of the leadership. Some exploit it for personal gain, they create wealth. Others leverage it for humanity. They build a network and make it work for their mission. The causes behind such leveraging determine the height of the leadership. (Published on LinkedIn on 7 February 2018. Got 165 Likes; 32 Comments and 8 Shares).

Glamour is a glittering appearance or talent or personality or behaviour of a person which gets extraordinary public attention, respect & recognition. The person becomes famous in public life with many fans and followers. Glamour is an attractive or exciting quality that makes certain people appealing. Bill Gates' glamour pulled Warren Buffet and later he donated $ 38 billion to Bill Gates's foundation for charity. Warren Buffet's glamour also attracted Bill Gates and he nurtured the relationship with Warren with great care. (as can be seen in the above photograph).

"Glamour is the magnet which creates the gravitational force around the leader. Glamour creates leader's sphere of influence from where his aura can be seen and felt. Glamour creates a 'halo-effect' around the leader and pulls people towards the leader. "

I can't think of a leader who didn't have glamour. People get pulled and love to stay with the glamorous leader. They enjoy the proximity to glamour. They enjoy the limelight. Glamorous people also get attracted to other glamorous people. During one of the interviews, Warren Buffet was asked about the greatest privilege that he enjoys. His response was, "I can meet any person I wish to meet."

"Glamour creates access for a leader so that he can reachout to the desired person or group. "

Warren created access to Bill Gates using his glamour. Bill Gates joined the board of directors of Berkshire Hathaway (Warren Buffet's company) when it was offered to him. Mr Bill Gates donated $ 28 billion to charity. The Gates get access to the richest people in the world due to their glamour. They have been travelling all over the globe and pursuing billionaires to donate money to charity. People listen carefully when glamorous people speak.

"Great leaders leverage their glamour for their mission. They multiply it by collaborative efforts. "

Bill Gates and his wife, Melinda, have taken up philanthropy as the mission of their life. Mr Gates is leveraging his glamour, creating access and providing collaborative leadership to handle certain adversities which are menacing humanity. This is what glamour can do to leadership and the leadership can do with glamour.

"Before getting glamour people run after it. After getting it they run away from it."

It usually happens to celebrities who get crazy fans. They become a nuisance for their hero. Their obsession to click a selfie with celebrities makes them do anything. Glamorous leaders have to observe a protocol in public life. Their fans make it difficult for them to follow the protocol. They invade privacy. Glamour changes the public relations game. But the great leaders don't run away from the glamour. They create a network, using their glamour, and make it work for their mission. Employees use the glamour of their leader as a float while exploring new areas of the markets or business. An 'entry ticket', created by the glamour of their leader, opens up many gates of opportunity for his organization.

"The fame of the leader becomes the major entry barrier for the competitors."

Competitors think twice before taking on a glamorous leader. They have to develop a concrete plan to overcome the power of his glamour. Smart competitors use his aura and work with him to gain favours for the entire industry from regulators like favourable tax structure, ease of regulation, de-licencing etc. The competitors acknowledge and respect the aura of such a leader and form industry associations under his leadership. These associations work as a pressure group and would even develop cartels for mutual benefits. Sometimes even regulators use the clout of glamorous leaders to bring industry leaders under one roof for a common cause. They also use it for gaining a competitive advantage in the international markets. Chinese are smartly using Jack Ma's glamour to gain an advantage in the American and in Indian markets. Political parties try to exploit the glamour of even religious leaders to influence the followers of their faith. The objective is to create a captive vote bank. Both, Baba Ramdeo and Prime Minister Modi are glamorous leaders. Their organizations try an all-out effort to create an aura around their personalities through systematic marketing campaigns. Thereafter they use the aura of these leaders in gaining advantages. Baba Ramdeo is the monk who created glamour. He did it through his genuine efforts to promote 'Yoga' and 'Pranayam'. He created the brand 'Patanjali' on a similar theme. He created a major threat to the global consumer packaging goods companies and FMCG companies in India. Baba Ramdeo is an example of how the leader transfers his glamour to the brand and fulfils his mission.

"Glamour is an impression which can even be better than reality."

Glamour and the 'Power of One' Some people become glamorous because of their formal position or profession. But great leaders create glamour around their position and chair. T N Sheshan created glamour around the position of the Chief Election Commissioner of India. He asserted the power given to the Election Commission by the constitution of India.

"Great leaders sharpen their weapons using glamour and the power of media."

The corrupt politicians felt threatened during T N Sheshan's tenure. His glamour emerged out of his courage to take on the might of the Indian politicians. The scene was clear. All Indian politicians were against Mr Sheshan but he over-powered them using the instruments and tools provided by the constitution,

"Great leaders demonstrate the 'Power of One' by creating and using glamour."

Mr Sheshan understood the power of glamour, he became media savvy and created glamour around his position. His success came out of his efforts to invest it in his mission to fumigate politics and free it from corrupt election practices. But for the glamour created around the position, Mr Sheshan couldn't have delivered what he contributed towards drastic improvements in the way the general elections are conducted in the largest democracy of the world. Before him and even today, the masses don't even know whether the Chief Election Commissioner of India is a male or female.

"Glamour has a natural tendency to breed jealousy. Glamorous leaders are objects of envy."

Glamour leaders are to be extra careful about their interactions. They can't step on the foot of people even unknowingly. If that happens then people's reactions can be harsher. Tiger Woods and Ameer Khan are the best examples. They were the victims of public wrath because of their glamour. Thus glamour can be a two-sided sword and needs training in handling it. Seasoned leaders handle it well. A new discipline in marketing can emerge,' Glamour management' The specialists can advise leaders on the various aspects of glamour. This discussion also highlights the criticality of the public relations (PR) exercise. After all management science recognizes PR as an important component of the promotional strategy. The marketing team can plan a detailed PR strategy keeping the leader and his/her glamour in the centre. PR should no longer be treated as only the cost centre. It can provide required dividends even in the short term.

Leader's Art of 'Super-human' Management

As machines replaced labor, the 'Personnel department' transformed into Human Relationship Management (HRM) department. With the emergence of the service economy, the 'high tech & high touch' approach became important. Talent got prominence. Attracting, retaining, and managing talent became the critical HRM activity. Talent Management is not just the modern avatar of HRM but there is more to it. It deals with managing the super-human. I call it Super-Human Relationship Management (SHRM). (Published on LinkedIn on 30 December 2017. Got 249 Likes; 67 Comments and 74 Shares).

The emergence of the service sector, the dominance of knowledge, and the increasing numbers of younger employees in the team made it essential to change the HRM approach. Knowledge became the power and the most valuable resource in the service economy. It replaced machines and materials as the most important resource from the production era.

Talent is the ability to do things right, the first time.

What is Talent? It is a natural ability or skill to do something. Usually, people learn by training or through an experience but talented people are the 'plug and play' type. Talent is natural it can't be acquired. Every family has an inheritance in the form of talent.

> *"Talent can't be manufactured. It can only be mined and can be processed further."*

Talent can be processed to make it suitable for a certain situation or for a certain team. It can be honed and polished to look professional. Talented people have different methods for acquiring knowledge. They can't be trained by the run-by-mill, regular training methods used for mediocre employees.

> *"A leader can be the best coach for talented employees rather than a trainer."*

Talented people prefer 'learning' rather than 'teaching'.They want to play an active role in the process of knowledge transfer. They evaluate the teacher before letting the teacher evaluate them. Sometimes they sound rebellious and arrogant due to their 'Out of the box' approach. But the great teachers are masters of training the talent. They possess the required talent, tact, and patience to train the talent. Phil Jackson is such a master coach who trained the all-time great basketball talents like Michael Jordon and Koby Braint.

> *"Experience sinks in, while talent sizzles out. Experience can be gained on the field but talent comes from the mother's womb."*

Talented employees can do certain things which others can't. Coaching and practice produce wonderful results for talent. But talented people require a talented coach. The practice provides confidence and develops self-belief.

"Talent comes to light by exposure and opportunity. A leader is an enabler for performing talent."

Leaders play a critical role in making talent work. They spot the talent and provide exposure and opportunity. Talent is sparkling. It glitters. Leaders get attracted to this. Leaders see talent when it is in infancy hence they develop the skill to judge it early, even before the talented person himself knows about it. Leaders educate talent and provide a sense of purpose. The talent starts contributing at its best only when the leader inspires it, fits it into the team, and provides the mission to the talented team.

"The leader's challenge is, how to discipline the talent, make it work in a team & make it contribute energy to his mission."

Talent and Focus Talented people are usually interested in many areas. They love multi-tasking which makes it difficult for them to focus on the task. Talent loves experimenting with new ideas. Scattered efforts wouldn't give focused results, hence the leader has to ensure that talent focuses only on the given task. Such discipline is critical for producing the required results.

"The leader has to put talent on track and prevent it from digressing."

Talent & Motivation Talented people are creative people. They are generally high on emotions. Their sensitivity makes them fragile. The leader and the team have to handle them with care or else they are demotivated. Some talented people lack motivation,

"The skill of leadership is to identify the greed of the talent and try to satisfy it. Leaders connect their greed to performance."

Some talented people are in the self-actualization mode. Their passion is to achieve excellence in their field. Other team members tend to look at it as a crazy idea but the search for excellence challenges and motivates talented people.

"The leader has to tune up the talent and the team for matching their frequency."

Talent and Teamwork Talented people have sharper perceptions. They comprehend the work situation faster. They feel frustrated by the slow pace of other team members. Their impatience creates human relations problems with other team players. Their expertise makes them do work much faster than others hence other people struggle to catch up with their speed. Others blame them as solo performers and criticize them for poor teamwork. In many organizations, talented people get secluded because others group against them. The leader has to educate talent and orient it to suit the organization's culture.

"Talented people invent methods, innovate approaches and re-engineer processes. They design special purpose tools which were not known earlier."

Talented people appear super-human. They do things faster, more accurately, and at a lesser cost. 'Out of the box' is their method. They are perfectionists in approach. Even their lowest performance is at a much higher level. Their vision gives them foresight.

"Talented people never blink both eyes together, hence never lose sight of their target."

They are gifted. They hardly crib for tools and weapons. They can turn any item into a weapon. Others can't hold their weapon. Their way becomes their 'style'. Others emulate their style. Others benchmark them and follow them. Talented people become natural leaders.

"Talent is in DNA. Practice and hard work make the talent glitter."

A few people are trained in childhood when learning and grasping are at their peak. At just six, Louisa Donovan's talent as a gymnast is attracting attention in Australia. This rising sports star competed in her first competition at the 'Women's Artistic Gymnastics junior judges invitational competition- 2017'. When she was just four Louisa was selected to train with Australia's top gymnasts. Louisa is currently being trained for nine and a half hours a week. She then spends every day increasing her strength by doing sit-ups, crunches, v-snaps, chin-ups, handstands, and cartwheels. She is so dedicated and loves training. She hardly misses a training session, only ever due to illness. In the Australian national competition, Louisa won two gold medals for her bar routine and vault and two silver medals for beam and floor. Her ambition was to represent Australia at the 2028 Olympics.

Leaders and their talent management skills The great leaders very well know the value of talent. They know that they can build their organization around talented people. But they have a different perspective on looking at talent. They know talent cannot work in isolation.

"Talent needs synergetic support from the other team members."

Great leaders know that talent is always raw, it has rough edges. They know that the talent has odd shapes and is required to be balanced on its center of gravity. They know that the talent will be stable only when it stands in the center of gravity. It will deliver the results only when it is stable and supported well by the tailor-made structure in terms of the team.

"Great leaders make the talent stand on its center of gravity"

Making talent stand on its center of gravity requires identifying the core needs of the talented people and satisfying them to the extent that it creates a 'wow' factor. Such a delight acts as a motivator for the talent. It boosts their morale and they get going to deliver the impossible. Polishing the talent requires grinding their rough edges. It requires opening up their mind to organizational realities and the team requirements. It requires coaching of the talent so that they do not step onto the foot of other team members knowingly or unknowingly.

"Great leaders have the talent to spot the talent. They choose only that talent that can fit into their values, culture and team dynamics. Leaders look for 'coachable talent'."

Sometimes talent goes down under because it gets adulterated by arrogance, vices, poor human skills, greed, lust, laziness, lack of ambition, lack of motivation, etc. Leaders understand that without talent the organization ushers mediocracy. A leader's job is to identify, attract, retain and make talent work with full force towards his mission and vision.

Leaders are masters of distilling and segregating adulterated talent. They use their aura to mesmerize talent, attract it, and make it malleable to forge it for the required organizational purpose and vision.

Talent and Creativity great leaders create situations conducive to creativity. They know talent blossoms in such a creative environment. They delegate power to talented people. Great leaders create a culture to learn by improving on their mistakes. They create a culture wherein people 'forgive mistakes but never forget the lessons learnt from those mistakes'.

In a nutshell, talent is the natural ability to do things right the first time. It can't be transferred but it can be trained to take out the rough edges and make it suitable for organizational values and culture. Leaders have a talent to spot talent. They can do it even before the talented person knows his/her talent. But grooming, training, and orienting the talent is the major leadership challenge. A leader has to ensure that the talent doesn't digress and focus on his mission. Additionally, the talent has a natural resistance from the mediocracy. Such people try to nullify the competitive edge of the talent by finding faults and grouping against talented people in the form of an informal organization. If this happens then the talent gets suffocated, couldn't deliver the result, and leaves the organization. A leader has to help talent to overcome it and gain the acceptance of the team. His success as a leader depends on how he forms a team of talented people and makes them work in a team on his mission. A leader has to take an active role in grooming talent. If he gets busy and couldn't spare time then mediocracy successfully develops a gap between the leader and the talent forcing the talent to leave the organization.

CHAPTER TWENTY-SEVEN

Recruitment: Missing a shot

Why do Goldman Sachs and Tata Administrative Services (TAS) conduct seven rounds of interviews during the recruitment process? What are they looking for? What do they access? How do they access it? Why are they so obsessed with eliminating the 'black sheep'? An insight into the great leaders' minds and their approach to selecting their team. (Published on LinkedIn on 30 September 2017. Got 637 Likes; 46 Comments and 57 Shares).

My super-bosses, the leaders, were very choosy about people. They always took disproportionately high time to make up their mind on the selection of any recruit. I used to get fed up with them for their repeated denial to select people for the positions which required immediate replacements. We would shortlist and recommend suitable people, but the leader would keep on rejecting them. We used to be pressed due to acute manpower shortages. As I grew in the organization and started reporting directly to the top leaders, I started getting an insight into their decision-making, particularly, the way they choose people. My leaders knew that they could manage if they miss the bull's eye when choosing a bank or investors or suppliers or dealers, or even customers. The decision can always be corrected by the right replacement. However, they cannot change their team. It stays with them.

"The mark of a successful leadership is the average number of years the team members stick to them."

Successful leaders know the fact that people do not leave the organization they leave their bosses. They leave their teams when they feel suffocated. They feel that way when the team dynamics get ruined. It gets reflected in their behavior. Such disgruntled people start flouting the discipline, often come late and leave exactly on time. Their unhappiness gets reflected in work. They avoid decision making, pass the buck.

"Employees leave when they lose faith in the mission and hope in the leadership."

The values and behavior of the other members affect the members of the team. They either inspire or damage the morale of others. They define the team dynamics. Therefore leaders are very careful in choosing the team members. They feel if one black sheep gets inducted into the team, it can spoil the whole team.

"Collective attitudes of the members of the team shape up the organizational culture."

Leaders know that like other business processes, the recruitment process is also subjected to errors in human judgment. They can accommodate certain other errors, but they want zero tolerance in rejecting the bad guy, the black sheep. They accept the elimination of suitable candidates rather than selecting the wrong guy. The leaders do not get limited by the current job description (JD) of a candidate. They go beyond JD. They take a long-term perspective. Leaders know very well that the profiles are fluid. They change frequently. There are many important areas of the profile of the candidate which are critical for evaluation during the recruitment.

> *"Leaders read candidate's profiles between the lines while others are busy reading the lines. They are concerned about the deletions rather than the additions."*

Leaders know well that what is obvious may not be apparent. They focus on the areas of the bio-data normally overlooked by others. They question a few deletions which are critical to identifying the values, beliefs, upbringing, and social groups of the candidate. For the leaders, the process of recruitment is more of a 'matchmaking' than selecting or rejecting anybody.

> *"Operational managers tend to over-emphasize the suitability of the profile for the current job description (JD)."*

Matchmaking in recruitment: The top leadership perspective Recruitment accuracy is one of the critical success factors for an organization. Great leaders consider the current JD as the 'looks' of the person. That is required for matchmaking, but they feel the matchmaking should go beyond just the 'looks' of a person. Matchmaking requires short-term and long-term perspectives. Short-term matchmaking involves matching the job description and profile of the person.

> *"There is never a perfect match. Companies have to arrive at the golden mean and find the best possible fit."*

In fact, the perfect matching between the JD and profile hardly leaves any room for job rotation. Such a 'perfect person' becomes the specialist & the team loses the flexibility to deploy the person for some other work.

He will be like 'a goalkeeper' in soccer who can only be given one role but the team has only one goalkeeper & it wants other members to be flexible.

Matchmaking beyond JD: A match is also required between the personal and the organization values. The candidate must fit into the organizational culture. He or she should also fit into the team based on her personality traits. The career objective of the person must match the mission & vision of the organization. Recruitment accuracy is the function of this critical matchmaking process. The corporate eagles jump at a fish in the ocean, only to realize that they completely missed the target or caught the wrong fish. In either case, it is a frustrating experience for the company & also for the employee. Great leaders have a radically different approach to recruitment and selection of employees. They do not believe in a half an hour interview. In their view, the candidates project the ideal image during such an interaction rather than displaying the reality. Leaders look at the interview behavior as party behavior. People want to be at their best when they are at a party.

> *"During the job interviews, candidates project what they want to be rather than what they are."*

Companies like Goldman Sachs or Tata Sons (for their Tata Administrative Services) conduct interviews in multiple rounds. They know that the person can be at his best on a specific day. They do not want to get influenced by that peak performance. They want to know the average or normal performance of a person. They have developed an expertise in accessing the person beyond his official CV. Goldman Sachs does not assess a CV, They assess a person. They know most of the time the person is missing from the CV. The multiple interview rounds provide an opportunity for people in the organization to look at the person from various angles. The HR team can figure out whether the person can be fitted into the organizational culture and values. The department bosses can find out whether he/she can be fitted into the 'sub-culture' of their team. They want to know what the person will bring to the team, and whether he would add some value. If yes, then in what way?

"Some companies conduct psychometric tests during the recruitment process. The success of a well-crafted psychometric test depends on the authentic and candid responses from the candidates."

Psychometric tests are a function of the culture. They work better in the Western world where the opportunities outnumber the candidates. They had serious limitations in the developing world because of the misgivings associated with them. Candidates mess up the psychometric and aptitude tests due to desperation. Candidates focus on the psychology of an evaluator rather than their own while responding to the tests.

"During the psychometric tests, the candidates tend to focus on the acceptable response rather than the right response."

Looking at the variables in the recruitment process & the uncertainties associated with them, organizations are required to focus on certain tools and technics. Such tools should be acceptable to the top leadership. The companies can follow these principles:

Catch them young Young employees are flexible and coachable. They can be molded well to suit the requirements of the team. They can adapt to the culture of the organization & also to the sub-culture of the team in which they work. They are ambitious and energetic with the advantage of physical energy. The organizations should create programs like an apprenticeship, graduate trainees, engineer trainees, and management trainees. The attrition among these groups is on account of the ill-treatment, and lack of learning and growth opportunities. If they are properly taken care of, then youngsters can develop a long-term perspective.

Create simulations Summer internships can be the simulation that can provide a better opportunity to see the person on the job. The critical selection should be made for internships & a candidate should be observed carefully during the internship.

Prefer the known devil Prefer salespersons working with your distributors. Also, the people who worked with the companies from whom you outsource manpower. The promotions should be made from within the organization rather than bringing seniors from outside. Some seniors also have the tendency to recruit people from their earlier organizations.

A close aide of the Indian business tycoon, late Shri Dhirubhai Ambani shared an interesting experience while working on the installation of one of the largest refineries in the world at Jamnagar in Western India. When Dhirubhai was given a proposal to recruit 1500 workers he asked to recruit 3000 workers & made them pay 3 months' salary. After 3 months he asked to retain the best 1500 workers and relieve others. This is how he ensured to induct only the best people leaving aside the 'black sheep'.

e can conclude that recruitment is an equally risky business process as any other critical process. Rather it is riskier than most processes. Great leaders provide their vision to convert it into a calculated risk. Great companies have developed great methods to ensure that they do not miss the target & recruit the black sheep. Great leaders & great companies go beyond CV & beyond matching it with their current profile. They successfully overcome the 'recruitment myopia' by taking a long-term perspective in the selection of every team member. There is a natural tendency to choose the 'known devil' hence students should work hard on their internships.

CHAPTER TWENTY-EIGHT

Why Do Leaders Get Up?

People were shocked when Jack Ma stepped down as Chairman of the board of Alibaba by handing over the management function to Daniel Zhang. They were surprised to see Jack getting up and getting out of the management when Alibaba locked horns with Amazon. Jack understood the leadership game better. He learnt it from the veterans like Warren Buffet, Robson Walton, and Bill Gates. They also handed over the management to their successors, whom they groomed, and preferred to remain owners. They understood the leadership role conceptually. (Published on LinkedIn on 20 September 2018. Got 242 Likes; 23 comments and 22 Shares)

People get confused between leadership and management. They think the leader is the head of the management. That may not be true. Many leaders are not a part of the management. Leaders have a definite role to play and it is distinctly different from the role of the management. Bill Gates, Warren Buffet, Larry Page (of Google), Robson Walton (of Walmart), Narayan Murthy, Ratan Tata, Harsh Mariwala & Jack Ma realized that the leader and management are two different things.

"Leaders value the mission more than the ownership of the organization."

Great leaders are identified by their commitment to the mission. They do anything and everything, within their value system for their mission. Jack Ma understood the effectiveness and efficiency of Daniel Zhang. Jack understood and strongly supported the theme suggested by Daniel, the 'New Retail'. Jack handed over the management function to Daniel by appointing him as the Chairman of the board. Jack preferred to remain, Director, even if he holds the majority equity stake in the Alibaba group company which has acquired a global scale under Jack's leadership. Warren Buffet was one of the first business leaders who understood this difference well. He identified a talented man, Ajit Jain, and handed over the management function to him. If you watch his interview on YouTube then you will get to see Warren singing praises for Ajit and rating him above Warren Buffet himself. Warren felt that his company would be managed better by Ajit. Warren remained owner but Ajit was made the head of the management team. Bill Gates was another visionary who realized the distinction faster. He handed over the leadership to Steve Ballmer rather than getting actively involved in the management function. After a few years, Steve also rode on Bill's wisdom and pushed himself away from the management function. Steve made the way for Satya Nadella, the current CEO of Microsoft who is heading the management team. One gets charged up by some idea or concept. It usually comes from one's passion. He/she wants to do something about the idea. Over a period of time, the idea crystallized, and then it gets refined. This refinement gives birth to the mission. One gets obsessed with the mission. He/she knows that a team is required to accomplish the mission. The person starts sharing the idea with others & searches for like-minded people. Some people who share the mission and start voluntarily following the mission. Thus the leader is born. A leader is somebody with whom people entrust power to control them.

"The leader lives for the mission. The leader develops the team for the mission."

A leader is the owner of the mission. He is also the owner of the future of his team. The leader entrusts the mission to the team whereas the team trusts their career to the leader. The bond between the leader and the team gets stronger as they entrust their most valuable aspiration to each other.

"The relationship between the leader and his team is always aspirational. Their expectations from each other are endless."

One team member crosses the threshold and goes near the leader's line of expectation. He becomes the leader's natural choice as a successor. They don't get up from the driving seat unless they find such a successor. The leader takes his own fine time to find the successor because he doesn't want to take a chance when it comes to the commitment to the mission.

"Great leaders value the level of 'commitment to the mission' as the decision-making parameter while choosing the successor."

Why do leaders get separated from management? Great leaders want to double the force for achieving the mission. The moment they find a team player who has high potential & commitment to the mission, they get up from their seat & make that person occupy the driving seat. They know such an act enhances the morale of the team player & he becomes even more committed to the mission. Secondly, leaders are obsessed with the 'outsider's view' of their organization. They love to see their organization from the customer's binoculars.

"The leaders love to look at their organization from the 'outsider's perspective'."

They want to see their organization as their customers see it. They also want to look at the organization from the perspectives of the different stakeholders like suppliers, channel partners, etc. Even the competitor's perspective is valuable to them. As long as they are leaders, they feel they tend to have a biased and defensive attitude toward the actions of the organization in the marketplace. When leaders separate themselves from management they can look at their organization objectively.

"Leaders want the mission to be organization-specific rather than the leader specific."

Great leaders know that the mission is shared only when the career aspiration is shared. They enjoy the process of developing other leaders who can make the organization stronger. Leaders create leaders primarily because the mission is the leader's ownership and the leader wants to multiply the force chasing the mission. Such leaders also care for the dreams of their team members like they care about their own dreams. They know leading the organization is the ultimate dream of ambitious team members and the leaders don't want to be a stumbling block.

"Leaders connect organizational mission to the dreams of their team members."

Great leaders project mission as the target and fulfillment of their personal dreams as rewards. By appointing the successor the leaders pass on the message that the deserving persons can even wear the leadership crown. Such a gesture enhances the morale of the senior members of the team. The energy gets created by triggering the leadership aspirations.

"The ultimate wisdom of the leader is in the realization that management, leadership, and ownership are distinctly different roles."

Management, Leadership, and Ownership Growing organizations have the owners looking after management, as a leader. As organizations grow, these three roles get separated. Owners own the organization financially and legally. The leader owns the mission and also the trust of the stakeholders.

"Owners provide resources, the leader provides the purpose and direction to the resources, and the management optimizes given resources and en-cashes them in multiples."

In order to be globally successful, all three institutions are required to be performing their tasks well. They are also required to work in tandem to create synergy.

What do leaders do after taking off the leadership crown? In Maslow's hierarchy of human needs, leaders reach the self-actualization stage. They go beyond recognition, esteem & money. Jack Ma says, " If you have $1 Million then it is your money but if you have $1 Billion then it is not your money. It is the trust of society with you." Watch the initial few minutes of this Youtube video. Different leaders react differently. Some pursue their passion. Some prefer to be team members. A few also become the protector and providers of the organization. They raise resources. Most leaders become virtual brand ambassadors for their companies. Some become coaches and train young members of the team. The great leaders get into philanthropy in a big way after they keep their reins down.

"After achieving the purpose of existence for their organizations, the great industry leaders find their own purpose in life, generosity and charity. "

Modern-day Robin Hoods Great industry leaders are modern-day Robin Hoods. They become the richest persons in the world of their talent, hard work, and wisdom supported by the blessings of God. Once they reach the top, they start philanthropy and charity. Warren Buffet donated $ 32 billion, Bill Gates donated $ 28.5 billion. Bill Gates also convinced many billionaires to donate billions of dollars. As Mr. Gates put it, these talented people use their talent to attract wealth & then they utilize this wealth for the less privileged people in the society like women and children in the developing world, poor, physically challenged people, etc. Some leaders embrace ecological causes. The Nobel Peace Prize for 2007 was awarded to former US Vice President Al Gore for his efforts to obtain and disseminate information about the climate challenge.

n a nutshell, great leaders develop a passion. Their passion takes them to their mission. They form a team and share their mission with the team. In the initial phase, they are the leaders, owners, and management as well. As the organization develops a scale, the ownership, leadership, and management get separated. Great leaders become owners and promote their deputy who is groomed well, as the leader. They also develop the team and delegate the management function to the team. Great leaders then change their roles. They hand over the leadership baton and remain owners. The owners arrange resources, the leader directs resources towards the mission with a sense of purpose. The management ensures optimum utilization of resources and their multi-fold growth. The great leaders become wealth creators. They generate the wealth and direct it to the needy, less privileged sections of society. Great leaders do a great job even after they get up from the leadership chair. They always remain role models for others in all stages of their life.

The Power of Delegation

Delegation is not just passing on the authority, it means enabling somebody to act. It is the method by which you acknowledge the potential of your subordinates and show trust in their competencies. It is the way to pass on the positive message and feelings about people. It is the process by which you help people to perform their jobs. People can feel the leadership better when the leaders delegate their authority to their people. Delegation develops your followers as the leader grows. The delegation also develops autonomy by empowering the employees. The team dynamics develop The 'Hands On' attitude of the team. It helps to make the organization 'Customer Centric'. (Published on LinkedIn on 15 July 2017. Got 68 Likes; 5 Comments and 85 Shares).

There are many commonly used but widely misunderstood words in management. 'Delegation' would certainly appear on the top of such a list of words. During one of my management development programs, I asked participants to write synonyms of the word 'delegation'. The objective was to find out their perception of delegation. A few of the words they wrote were: transferring, passing on, partying away authority and responsibility, etc.

"Delegation is empowering, enabling, or entrusting."

Delegation is not just passing on the authority, it means enabling somebody to act, and empowering somebody to accelerate. It is the method by which you acknowledge the potential of your subordinates. It also means showing trust in their competencies. It is the way to pass on the positive message and feelings about people. It is the process by which you help people to perform their jobs.

"Delegation grows the human capital and the skill inventory by providing exposure, opportunity and training."

Delegation: An On-the-Job Training Method Delegation is helping your subordinate to grow. It is grooming of your team-mate to take up higher responsibility. It provides exposure to the person. It is a method to train your subordinates on the job. They develop knowledge and skills. They become confident. It is setting up a stage for the promotion. The leader can identify the level of acceptance of the person by the team. It is the simulation of a future leadership scenario. If the person performs after the delegation then he/she can be given the promotion. Delegation is a way to develop empathy When you delegate, your subordinates have to think like you think while making decisions. They start understanding your situation and your position. They understand you better.

"Delegation is a clever leadership style to develop the heart of the leader."

People can feel the leadership better when the leaders delegate their authority to their people. Leaders can develop stronger bonds using this technic.

Growing by Delegating: Delegation is growing by giving up. It not only helps the person who gets the power but also helps the one who shares it. Unless you delegate your existing authority how can you get the higher authority? When you are required to delegate the current role indicates that you are eligible for the higher role, you have grown organically, you need to face the more challenging tasks. It is the recognition that you have proved your ability in the present role, grown bigger than your shoes, and also shown the potential to lead the person who will do your current role.

"Holding on to power, too long, can be a boomerang, it can spoil your chances of getting promoted."

Becoming indispensable will neither let you go on leave nor allow you to grow to the next position. Seniors will be worried to promote you if they do not see the right replacement for you. Hence delegation is required in your vested interest. Many outstanding performers get stuck in their careers because they fail to develop their replacements, internally. Unless you have followers you can't be a leader.

"Delegation develops your followers and you become the leader."

Delegating powers and developing subordinates clears a path for promotion and improves your image as a team player. The team holds you high as a leader. The management looks at you as a team builder.

Building Teams by Delegation The strong team is always built on the noble intentions of the leader. The team looks at the delegation as your attempt to share power. They receive it well and respond positively with equal force.

"A delegation is a tool for building a strong team."

Delegation develops belongingness. The person feels the responsibility and the expectations of the leader. The person gets motivated because the recognition is given to him. It also sends a message about succession. The team gets prepared, mentally, for the change of leadership.

"Great leaders make themselves redundant by developing other leaders who have the capability to replace them."

The Art of Delegation It is more of an art than science. One must know what to delegate, whom to delegate, how to delegate, how much to delegate, and when to delegate. There is no standard formula or equation. Delegation can be susceptible to mistakes. The wrong choice of a person, too much delegation, and a lack of performance standards and audits can develop power centers. It can demoralize other team members.

> *"The delegation must be based on fair parameters and followed by appropriate coaching by the leader himself."*

The person must get the benefit of the experience of his boss. It reduces his cost of learning and organizational loss. The leader has to exercise patience and tolerance during the initial phases of delegation. If not, then the subordinate would hesitate to make decisions and the purpose of delegation gets defeated. Delegation fails in an insecure environment. Trust, security, training, cooperation, and coordination can only boost the results after delegation. The person must see delegation as an attempt to help him develop leadership skills. If he develops an attitude that delegation is an attempt by the management to exploit him then the exercise becomes a mega failure. It should also not be seen as an attempt to pass on the blame or put somebody in a fix.

> *"Delegation can be successful with noble intentions, apt selection, and innovative methods of implementation."*

The timing of delegation is also critical. It should precede the time the person gets eligible for the next promotion. When the person performs well then he/she should get a promotion at the right interval. The team should see the elevation as a reward for the apt performance in the higher position, without the required designation and formal authority. It should be seen as the regularization of the deserving designation, remuneration, and powers. Delegation should create a chain reaction. The person who gets additional responsibility and powers must share his current responsibilities and powers with other team players.

> *"Great leaders use delegation as an effective tool to develop team dynamics and bonding."*

The art of delegation develops a 'Scalar chain' which is the important principle of management as stated by Henry Fayol. A delegation also develops autonomy by empowering the employees. The team dynamics develop The 'Hands On' attitude of the team. It helps to make the organization 'Customer Centric'.

Leading: From Maximum to Optimum Mindset

In the rat race for maximizing profits and sales, companies forget the flip side and the damages are created. Wise leaders focus on identifying the interests of all the stakeholders. (Published on LinkedIn on 13 July 2017. Got 42 Likes: 1 Comment and 25 Shares)

In economics, they believe that 'more and more you have something, lesser and lesser you feel, to have more of it.' Sometimes I doubt this 'law of diminishing marginal utility' Seniors want more when you deliver more. Additionally, they want more profits when you deliver more growth. They want a higher market share when you deliver more sales. Even if you deliver more sales, profits, and market share, they would punch you for the customer satisfaction index. There is a rat race for profit-maximizing, sales growth, market share, and customer satisfaction. In the corporate world, maximization can be an obsession. The only exceptions are cost and salaries. Hahaha, It is like that famous joke about what is the best life. The best life is having a German car, an American salary, a Japanese wife...... etc... Hahaha. Most of the time maximum remains only a dream. It remains on the paper.

"The Science of Management revolves around optimizing."

Trying to maximize metrics with different parameters of performance can be impossible. All values can't be maximized. Higher values of some parameters will push down the values of other parameters. We may not afford to have values of certain parameters below a specific level. Arriving at the golden mean which allows achieving the highest possible values of the critical parameters along with minimum required values of other essential/ desirable parameters is called optimization. For example, sales and market share can't be maximized because of the requirement of achieving a minimum level of profits.

"Leaders are masters of optimization"

They know which are the critical parameters, which are desirable and essential. Their wisdom tells them when and how the importance of the parameters changes. They judge the situation well and decide which parameters should be focused on and which need not. The process by which the leaders give up desirable and essential parameters to acquire optimum values of the critical parameters is called Trade-off. They use their gut feel, education, and experience to decide the optimum level of each parameter. They steer their organizations accordingly.

"Successful leaders know what should be traded off, when, how, how much, and against what."

Such leaders have an ability to identify what is core and what is required. They know what is critical and what is desirable. They trade-off only non-core parameters and are very stubborn on the core.

"Great leaders never trade off discipline for the performance or loyalty of an employee."

Great leaders do not let their people run for maximum. They know it is a rat race and even if they win they will be a rat. The Law of Physics states that any odd structure can be made to stand without any external support if it rests on its center of gravity. This law is also applicable in the corporate world.

"Great leaders identify the 'center of gravity' and make the organization rest on it."

The center of gravity is the point where all critical parameters provide optimum values. Organizations that rest on the center of gravity are successful organizations. They are the leaders in the market and they lead their industry. Great leaders are never obsessed bout the maximum. They want optimum. This ability of the leader makes the organization deliver the required result.

"The Center of gravity of the company is the optimum sales, profit, and market share."

I always wondered why the RPM meter was provided on the dashboard of a car. My friend educated me and taught me how to get the optimum fuel efficiency by maximizing the speed at a particular RPM. The leaders monitor the RPM of the organization by controlling the throttle (resources). Then they try to maximize the speed (growth) by appropriately steering to gain the optimum performance in terms of the top line and the bottom line. The optimum solution is a relative concept. What is optimum for a company may not be optimum for another company. The optimum solution is a function of a situation and organizational resources.

"The optimum solution is dynamic. It changes with time"

The changes in the macro-environment change the optimum value of different parameters. Leaders are required to constantly scan the environment and maintain the optimum solution. They need to be demanding and focus on the exchange while trading off the non-core parameters.

Flexing Reflexes: The Ultimate Leadership Skill

Decision-making on reflexes is an important skill in leadership and management. It can be developed with a lot of training and practice. The leaders should facilitate their employees in such a decision-making process. Wherein the employees get trained and empowered to make spontaneous decisions in response to the business stimuli. Decision-making on reflexes, with lightning speed, will mark successful **organizations.** (Published on LinkedIn on 2 May 2012. Got 50 Likes; 4 Comments and 2 Shares)

The pace of response is becoming more and more significant activity in modern-day business management. Competitors are becoming sharper, pre-emptive and so swift that they hardly provide any response time. Markets are extremely sensitive and volatile. The fund managers have to respond in the blink of an eye, or they lose millions. The HR professionals have to be on their toes. The talented employees are becoming demanding and impatient, thanks to their economic/peer pressures and the danglers offered by the competitors. Response time and speed of response will be critical. You do not have time to analyze, deliberate, formulate the problem, take consensus, and then initiate the response. Your actions must be reflexive. Corporate leaders have to train and empower professionals to flex their reflexes and deal with business stimuli on their reflexes, without losing out any time.

> *"The only way out is to improve the pace of response with accuracy and gravity."*

The dictionary defines reflexes as, 'an action that is performed without conscious thought as a response to a stimulus.' In business, there are many stimuli. Some are generated by customers; some are by competitors and the rest are by the business environment which surrounds the business. In the good old 'license era' the governments controlled the supply and demand side, under the pretext of 'fair allocation of the resources.'The Stimuli were fairly certain. Businesses could forecast, and plan accordingly. The business managers could do conscious thinking, deliberations, brainstorming, etc. The government operated on the advice of the planning commission which prepared a concrete (rather rigid) plan for the five years. Today that is a luxury. Modern-day managers are not that lucky. Businesses are volatile. Plans are rolling. For every performance ratio, there are mostly two denominators, cost and more than that, time. Even the government has done away with the model of 'planned economy. The planning commission became a dinosaur.

> *"Today the corporate philosophy is 'let the river come and we will cross it'."*

Today's business stimuli are like 'Reaction Ball, 'a favorite training tool. It is used to improve reaction time and agility in sports. The ball is not shaped like a sphere. It bounces quickly and unevenly. Athletes (as seen in the picture) use the ball during training by jumping it hard and attempting to catch it, which is difficult because the ball bounces unpredictably and quickly. It improves agility, hand-eye coordination, and fast reaction times. The markets are becoming equally bouncy and unpredictable. Business executives have to struggle with two bouncing balls, the 'Topline' (Sales), and the 'Bottomline' (Profits). Catching up with these reaction balls is quite a task. The worst part is that there is somebody ready to catch it even if you don't.

"No opportunity is lost, competitors will grab it"

Managers are required to be alert. They should have an open mind with no prejudices. They can't be making pre-recorded decisions. They need to develop an ability to sense and analyze any stimulus quickly and make a tailor-made response, ready in no time. They need to develop decision-making skills like martial art. The actions in martial arts are based on intuition and the sixth sense. It is a game of the subconscious mind which becomes more powerful than the conscious mind. If managers have to take decisions without conscious thoughts then they need to perfect the art of decision making and also the domain knowledge. Acting on the subconscious mind needs deeper domain knowledge, higher experience, honed skills along with sharp perceptions and empathy, full confidence and commitment, and a sense of belongingness to a team on the mission. Remember how you learned to drive? When you started, you were driving with a conscious mind, keeping track of road conditions and parameters specific to the car. When you mastered the driving skill then you drive with the subconscious mind while listening to music or chatting with friends. Corporate leaders have to design the training programs like sports coaches or martial art trainers. The focus has to be on developing skills of the highest order so that they can do it with a subconscious mind. The training of soldiers is not enough. Business executives need training like rare commandos, and 'Navy Seals' who carry out surgical strikes with extreme perfection.

"What can be some of the guiding principles? Martial arts can provide great insights into training reflexes. We can learn from their principles."

Don't Take Your Eyes Off Remaining alert and keeping track of every stimulus is important in martial arts. One can't be caught napping. My generation boasted about the ability to 'switch on and off,' keeping work and life separate, not letting them encroach on others' territory. But today's situation is different. In the globalized world, your Saturday can be customers' Friday. The stock market may collapse on your Sunday because it is already Monday in some other market.

"Gone are the days of work-life balance. Integrating work and life is important"

Working from home, working from the baseball stadium, working while commuting, and working from the cinema hall will be the order of the day. The place value of the work is diminishing. Companies realize the futility of the physical presence at a workplace Similarly the concept of weekdays/weekends, and working/non-working hours will also vanish. That doesn't mean people will be so workaholics. It means the compartments will disappear. The office will look like homes and homes will resemble offices, the work will be on clouds (digital), and meetings will be virtual, on conference calls or video conferencing, thanks to 4G and 100 MBPs networks.

"Emerging corporate culture is people socializing on weekdays and working for a few hours even on weekends and on vacations."

It will ensure that the managers will be hands-on. They won't miss any business opportunities. At the same time, they shall not be away from their family for days. This development is critical for developing reflexes in businesses. The organizations will respond swiftly to even a minor stimulus.

Reduce Reaction Time In martial arts it is a perception of the attack. One should try to reduce the time lag between the stimulus and the beginning of the response. It can happen when leaders develop the perception of their team. The faster the human immune system recognizes the type of virus, the better it is for the brain. It can order WBCs accordingly, and the body can produce the required protein to fight the infection. Perception can be developed through various methods. The more effective way is to provide exposure and opportunities to employees at an early age.

"Successful companies are getting younger and maintaining their speed and agility. Younger companies will have better reflexes."

Companies like Alibaba have average age employee age 27. Better coordination and cooperation through higher team spirit and opportunities to work in cross-disciplines are other enablers of reduced reaction time. How quickly you respond to the stimulus is an important part of reflexes.

Improve Speed of Response How quickly your organization moves from the trouble is important but how fast you move is equally important. The rate at which you take yourself out of the danger zone will define the quality of your reflexes.

"Collective wisdom will be very useful in developing pace by reducing inertia."

Delegation and empowerment will define the speed. The very concept of reflex action is a parallel decision-making system in the human body. It is triggered by the sensory system when a quick response is required to the extent that there is very little time available for the to and fro communication with the brain. Probably the best example of delegation and empowerment. Successful corporate leaders develop such parallel decision-making systems to take care of 'bouncing balls', and uncertain and unpredictable business stimuli.

Beware of the Back-kick The worst part of the reflexes is the back-kick. The stimulus can create a response that is exactly opposite to the expected action. Just like the action as shown in the adjacent picture where the patient involuntary and nearly instantaneous kicks the doctor in response to a stimulus given by him during the medical test. A few employees might try to ride the system in absence of the close monitoring by the senior team.

They earn a bad name for the concept of 'work from home'.

> *"A few employees neither work nor remain at home when expected to work from home"*

They do it even during weekdays and during office hours. The challenge for the leadership is dealing separately with such elements without harming the spirit of the team. Smart leaders do not throw the baby out with the bathwater. Decision-making on reflexes is an important skill in management. It can be developed with a lot of training and practice. The leaders should facilitate their employees in such a decision-making process. Wherein the employees get trained and empowered to make spontaneous decisions in response to the business stimuli. Decision-making on reflexes, with lightning speed, will mark successful organizations.

No Does Not Mean Never

It is important to learn to say and also to receive 'No' in life. How and when to say No is an art. Handling No is a part of wisdom. No may not be a hurdle. It can be a foundation of innovation. (Published on LinkedIn on 1 July 2017. Got 61 Likes; 9 Comments and 45 Shares)

Even a fool can say 'Yes' but it requires a man of wisdom to say 'No'

I have realized that people really struggle hard with the word 'No'. They mess up when required to deny something to someone. They feel nervous to say no. Some feel guilty to say no. Some people need to gather the courage to say no. They keep postponing their communication.

"'No' is a weapon. Requires training in handling"

Some people say 'no' in haste. Some people take their fine time and search for the right opportunity. Under the pressure, people tend to forget the soft skills required to deliver the word 'No'. It is a two-sided sword that requires proper training to handle or else it can harm the person handling it.

"'No' is the most difficult word to say because it needs three things tongue, heart, and brain"

Why is it so tough to say no? Could be because certain fears are associated with this word or because of the ripple it creates. It can be demoralizing. It can hurt. You may lose a chance. It can spoil relationships. It can lead to anger or a cry. It hits equally hard for kids, men, women & elderly people. The only difference is the reaction pattern of a person who gets hit by 'No'. The way people react depends on their personality and also on their eagerness to get 'Yes'. It hits harder when it misses mounted hopes and emotions. It can be a real destroyer when the stakes are higher. The loss can be monetary or emotional. It can be actual or virtual. "No" can be really nasty.

"'No' is difficult to deliver because it is more difficult to receive."

Neither the giver nor the receiver likes it. Both hate equally. Both feel that there would be a 'lose-lose' proposition associated with it. The receiver feels frustrated because of the perception that he reached a dead end. The one who delivers gets the bad taste because of the negativity it generates. In management and while leading, one can't get rid of 'No'. In fact, the higher & higher you grow on the organizational ladder more & more you are required to say no. It is an antibiotic that may cause a reaction, and may cause side effects but still requires to be delivered wherever required.

'No' is also the shield. It can protect you from embracement, humiliation, and even punishments. Some people hide behind 'no' because it is the safer bet. It is a roadblock.

> *"'No' is a source of innovation."*

Successful leaders do not treat 'no' as a hurdle. They circumvent it. It challenges creative minds because people are forced to develop another way or method. Successful leaders don't feel dejected. They get charged. They learn to use 'no' as a springboard to bounce back. How to handle 'No' when you have to deal with it? I can think of some ways based on my experience and observations.

> *"The best treatment is 'cure without medicine'"*

Skip the decision point Do not reach a situation that has either a 'Yes' or 'No' decision point. Good leaders involve their team in all aspects of management and decision-making. They provide the total picture. As a result, the team members get the context and know the constraints. They can empathize with the leader. They know what is possible and what is not. Hence they do not seek any yes/no decision from the leader.

Delegate Experienced leaders know the power of delegation. They develop members of their team and teach them decision-making. Give them exposure and the opportunity to make decisions. They support team member when his/her decision goes wrong. They Educate the decision maker rather than a curse for the error. Good leaders know very well that,

> *"Delegation is the only way to get freedom from routine and operational work."*

The leader can grow only by delegation. A delegation of power is also the delegation of the responsibility to say 'No'. Then the devil, called 'No', starts chasing the new guy.

Develop alternatives The word 'No' hurts more when the person receiving it does not have an alternative to fall back upon. The gravity of the hurt gets lowered when the person realizes that he can have his way by using some other method or technic. Alternatives show possibilities and the person doesn't feel that he is stuck and hit the dead end.

How to say 'No'? How to say 'no' is an art. Great leaders do not say it categorically or explicitly. They don't even show facial expressions. they know how other things can be more powerful than plain and simple 'no'.

> *"Great leaders say 'no' through their body language. They say it through their silence."*

The great leaders know that 'no' can be a very strong expression of disapproval. It can be demoralizing and damaging. They know that a 'no' can be interpreted as a denial of opportunity or the medium for discrimination or a strong bias or prejudice. The tone and style of saying no matter a lot. Some people deliver 'no' with a sugar coating. They prepare the other person for receiving a 'no'. They try to give a preamble that explains the logic behind 'no'.

> *"How you say 'no' to somebody determines your future relationship with that person"*

The time is right Untimely 'no' creates havoc. One has to develop patience and wait till his turn comes. Don't slam 'no' when the other person is already struggling with other issues and your 'no 'could act like the last straw on the camel's back. Use your procrastination skills to buy the required time. Provide feelers so that the person. Let him develop a gut feeling that your reply will be 'no'. At the same time do not say 'no' when the person is celebrating something and is overwhelmed with joy.

> *"God always compensates when he says 'no' to somebody"*

Post Delivery Behavior Empathize with a person to whom you said 'no'. Try to compensate with something else, if you can. Take initiative in maintaining the relationship. Create some opportunity to say 'yes'. Two consecutive 'no's can destroy the person and your relationship is likely to go for the toss. He starts developing the feeling that you may not say yes to anything he proposes in the future.

Encash the guilt If you are on the wrong side and received somebody's 'no'. Then you can try to get mileage out of it. The person, having said 'no' to you, develops guilt. Encash the guilt. Try to minimize the damage caused by his 'no'. Prudent managers leverage 'no' to maximize their gain in some other areas. They take the support and help of the same person who threw 'no' at them. Such an approach is very useful in selling products or services.

"The selling profession exists because people have a tendency to say 'no'."

Persuasion is considered the best quality for a salesperson. It starts with 'no'. Every sales professional must keep in mind that the root cause behind their employment is 'no' of the customers. Their job is managing 'no'. Salespersons must remember that

"No does not mean never"

The main distinguisher between success and failure is the ability to understand the word 'no', read the context behind it, minimize the damage caused by it, and leverage it to create an advantage in business.

CHAPTER THIRTY-THREE

Political Leadership: What They Don't Teach You at Harvard

Corporate leadership certainly has its own set of challenges but Political leadership offers higher rigor, risk, and challenges. Politicians have to deal with many more variables, stakeholders, and complex situations. They have to hit harder targets. Political leadership has to deal with running and intermittently invisible targets. The worst part of a political career is not having formal training. This article discusses these challenges. (Published on LinkedIn on 8 July 2017. Got 55 Likes; 4 Comments and 41 Shares.)

Churchill once said, "Democracy is the worst form of government except for all other forms". I am sure he said it after experiencing the challenges as the leader of a democratic government. In fact, He was among the fortunate leaders. He led the government in the majority, These days many national leaders are not so lucky. They have to form and lead coalition governments. Leading such governments is quite a challenge. Corporate leadership certainly has its own set of challenges but Political leadership offers higher rigor, risk, and challenges. Politicians have to deal with many more variables, stakeholders, and complex situations. The cost of their mistakes is higher. They have to climb stiffer slopes and hit harder targets. If corporate leaders have to hit moving targets, political leadership has to deal with running and intermittently invisible targets.

"The worst part of a political career is not having a formal training"

Most of the time the corporate leaders are thoroughly trained either formally or informally. The B-schools train them in the classrooms and companies train them on the job. They learn through simulation techniques and case studies which help them to learn from others' experiences and at the organizational/parental cost. Looking at the successful political leaders I always wonder can we produce such leaders in B-schools? Political leaders are not that lucky.

"Politicians can't go to a B-school to learn leadership. They learn only through their own experience and by paying a heavy cost."

They learn leadership the hard way. Their learning method is 'experiential learning. Who are their teachers? Voters, party leadership/workers, and political and legal systems teach politicians. Parliament, assembly, and constituency are their learning halls. Elections are their examination. The opposition, press, judiciary and most importantly the public perception evaluate them. Their success in the exam raises them to power, a failure may land them in jail. Recently, I was having a family chat with my uncle. He was a minister since he was 28. Worked for three decades, as a minister, with the Maharashtra state government. He also headed the state government as the Chief Minister. It was a coalition government. He worked as one of the most senior Ministers of the Govt of India. It was also the coalition government.

He was the leader of the ruling party in the Lok Sabha. Powerful credentials to opine on the leadership in the government. I was enjoying his leadership experiences and wisdom while trying to draw the lessons for corporate leadership. I am penning down what I could comprehend.

Leading and Managing Dual Organizations Corporate leaders deal with huge structures and many employees but they have a single organization to deal and everybody is on the payroll. Political leaders have to manage two organizations and deal with the team which is not on their payrolls.

Political leaders have to run two organizations parallelly, the formal bureaucracy of the government rank and files and also the informal organization of the party workers. Both of these are radically different organizations requiring heterogeneous leadership skills.

Motivating and leading both of these organizations of protected/pampered bureaucrats and non-salaried party workers is equally challenging. A successful political leader has to succeed in both of these organizations.

Managing the Press and Judiciary In a democracy press can catch you napping. The judiciary can hit you hard. Managing them is the key to success. Successful politicians keep themselves away as far as possible. When they are required to deal with these forces they exercise petitions, tolerance, and modesty. They avoid overstatements and prefer to keep a low profile. An attempt to outfox them can land you in great trouble.

> *"Successful politicians are masters of managing the press and avoiding the judiciary."*

The state governments have to manage central government machinery since they control resources. The problem gets complicated when the opposition party rules the central government. The same problem is faced by the central government while dealing with the state governments in the areas where the Constitution has empowered the state governments

Managing the Opposition Politicians have to remember that the opposition is not an enemy. They represent different political ideologies and faith. They have different political organizations and leadership.

Rising to power doesn't mean irradiation of the opposition. They form an important pillar of democracy and are required to be treated with respect.

"Prudent politicians know that today's opposition is tomorrow's ruling party. They use power to oblige opposition party members rather than destroy them."

I have seen our uncle sharing personal friendships with many opposition leaders who frequent his office and residence. He would never say 'no' to any personal request made by his opponents. They also obliged him when he required their support for personal or political reasons. They use to criticize him on public forums for political reasons but shared very good personal chemistry. His 75th birthday celebrations were attended by more opposition leaders than his own party leaders.

Managing Coalition These days it became increasingly difficult to form a government on your own party strength. Political parties are required to form coalition governments. Forming such a government required trust and goodwill among other political parties. The coalition must accept your party agenda and your party leadership. Running a coalition government needs a different set of skills. One should have tolerance and patience along with an ability to negotiate hard and cut a deal. Great leaders have the ability to trade-off. They know what, when, how, and how much to trade off.

"Coalition leaders are masters of blowing hot and cold. They have to maintain their identity while running the government."

Successful coalition leaders maintain pressure on their partners but it is well within the elastic limit. They would never stretch it to the yield point.

Implementation Skill Citizens are getting increasingly demanding about their rights and they expect the government which delivers the result. Successful political leaders know very well what works and what doesn't. They never overpromise.

"Successful political leaders raise the hopes of people and deliver the results"

They know the systems and people so well and guide the bureaucracy to find the way out through any difficult impasse. They wouldn't come under the scanner of the media or under the clutches of the judiciary. They share personal relationships within and outside the government and have the ability and willingness to leverage it. They identify and plan for all the stumbling blocks on their way to successful implementation.

Fund Raising Skill With increasing inflation and changing the culture, political parties are requiring more and more funds. They have to manage the huge network of party workers. Fighting elections require a lot of money. Successful political leaders know how to raise funds. They know whom, how, when, and how much to ask. They know how to return the debt by not coming under the media scanner or under scam.

Networking Skills Political leaders have good networking skills. They identify people of substance and develop rapport. They are masters of leveraging their contacts. They have friends in all the fields and they leverage their connections for their political agenda and for their constituency. Anybody who has leadership aspirations has to develop these skills. These skills are equally useful in political and business careers. They are the distinguishers of successful leaders. Corporate leaders develop them in the labs and political leaders grow them in the field.

CHAPTER THIRTY-FOUR

I Don't Agree. But... I Accept

Concludingbrainstorming sessions are always difficult. Initially, we love the differences that emerge out of discussions but then the going gets tough when people stick to their viewsand& don't budge. Some differences are impossible to bridge. What should be done in such cases? (Published on LinkedIn on 15 November 2015. Got 38 Likes; 13 Comments and 48 Shares)

"When two men in a business always agree, one of them is unnecessary....... If they do not agree on anything, both of them are unnecessary."

Some managers have a habit of working with like-minded people. They like those who think like them. Managers argue that such conviction is very necessary to bring the required results. The question is, whether it is a shared view or just a reflected view. Is it genuine agreement or professional hypocrisy? Great minds think alike but great organizations were always built by a team of people who had many disagreements. They agreed to disagree.

Disagreement Management

Disagreements are functions of many variables. The most important variable is perception. It is the process by which we attach meanings to things around us. It is the way in which we understand the outside world.

Different people understand the world differently hence they have different perceptions. Different perceptions lead to different views and hence disagreements. Perception is a function of intelligence, upbringing, and experience. One has to develop the right perception in order to understand the other members of the team. Another variable that can develop agreement is empathy. It is an ability to get into somebody else's shoes. It develops an understanding of other person's views and slowly develops telepathy with that person. Values differ resulting in disagreements. Many times disagreement is the outcome of value conflict. Great organizations develop collective values. Different attitudes lead to differences of opinion. Perception, empathy, values, and attitudes are deep-rooted and difficult to change. People find it difficult to reach an agreement with others having a different set of said variables. Organizations give great emphasis on these variables, in the selection process. They know these variables are 'given' and they can hardly change them.

Differences in the context can also lead to disagreements. Training, consulting, good listening, and exchanging information can develop the required context.

Different Thinking - Different Possibilities

Any team would require members who have divergent thinking. It helps in identifying different variables and their possible behavior. Those who think differently see different possibilities, and develop different solutions, and different alternatives. The team gets benefited from more options at their disposal.

Collective wisdom

The strength of any relationship always depends on how do people manage their differences. Connecting the positive terminal to the negative facilitates the flow of electricity and converts chemical energy to electric energy. Creating energy in the organization also needs connecting people with different charges. They all contribute to the pool of energy. One of the difficult tasks of the leader is to create collective wisdom in the organization. A leader's wisdom must be the seed of such collective wisdom. A leader should refine his wisdom by blending it with others.

Power of democracy

Right to differ is the power of democracy. But this boon is becoming a curse. Disagreement is not only a corporate problem. With the advances in education, increasing exposure, and tools like the internet more and more people are thinking independently. Consensus is becoming difficult. Globally more and more governments are coalition governments. Political parties are disintegrating. Local parties, with different viewpoints, are making inroads into national politics. Joint families are disintegrating, nuclear families are also shrinking and making way for singles. The divorce rate is on rising. The foundation of this crisis is 'disagreement'. Indians visiting China see the remarkable progress achieved in just a couple of decades. We are thinking hard about the present model of our democracy. The biggest failure of Indian politicians is to forge national consensus and create collective wisdom on many critical issues of development.

I do not agree but I accept

One may not agree with the collective wisdom of the organization but one has to trade off one's stubborn stand for consensus. One would say... "I do not agree but I accept." In globalized organizations with cross-cultures, this spirit is very important. It can facilitate delegation and autonomy. Seniors will be comfortable in giving up their controls only when they know that their subordinates will accept certain things even if they do not agree. It helps in developing trust. Loyal employees are those who fight during planning but unite during execution. That makes a winning team or else an organization may be democratic but bankrupt.

Learning to compete in unfair environment

Leaders know that there is no point in complaining about the unfair environment. In every Market, there will be a few competitors who will have certain unfair advantages. The leadership challenge is how to nullify them. (Published on 17 August 2017. Got 19 Likes; 1 Comment and 6 Shares).

When it comes to performing in a tough environment people often complain about the lack of a level playing field. The tough environment may not be an unfair environment. When they say unfairly they mean different things. Unfair could mean not equal. Nature is all about inequality. No two faces are the same. No two fruits taste the same. Even the intensity of the fragrance of two similar flowers differs. In my opinion, equality is an unnatural concept. It is a concept created by humans. Anything which is unnatural is doomed to fail in the long term. Nature has also given us many tools and instincts to fight out inequality hence one should focus on leveraging them rather than complaining about the inequality. Take an example of beauty. Can you really define it? In some cases, beauty is sharp features or complexion or good shape or the skin or hairstyle or height or the smile or the aura of talent glowing on the face. In most cases, beauty is a combination of two or more of the above things. Any beauty specialist will advise you to highlight what you have rather than worrying about what you do not have. In nutshell, no two beautiful ladies look alike. They are unequal but still beautiful. Unfair could also mean not being in the line with the expectations. In case of feeling unfair when things are not in the line of expectation, one should first check the expectations. Maybe expectations are not fair or there are over expectations. In such a case we are the source of the trouble and not the environment. It is our failure to predict irrespective of the environment. Unfair could also mean biased, a preference for one over another. Just change the hat. Think differently. when you are the decision maker and you have to choose between unknown, ill-known, and well-known what will you do? Many times only a certain number of people are to be selected from among a list of many eligible persons. The other person could have been preferred over you because of many possible reasons like the comfort level of the selector, expected attrition, or the cost. You may be over-qualified and somebody may be just qualified enough. They do not want to use a sword for the work of a pin. The bias may not be negative. The rejection could be only on the basis of the miss-match between the requirement and your profile. Stop reading too much in rejection. It could be a harsh word and a demoralizing phrase. Just treat it as a non-inclusion and get over it. There is no point in complaining about an unfair environment.

What makes the environment tough? Sometimes the environment can be tough, if not unfair. That makes it so tough? Peer pressure, family aspirations, social status, and a false sense of recognition can make the environment tough. These factors may push the expectations to an impossible level. They will create friction and generate heat which would be difficult to sustain.

How to cope with it? There may not be a standard way to deal with the tough or unfair environment however some tips can be very useful.

Learn to stay with the problem We may not be in a position to solve all the problems we encounter. Some will be beyond our reach. They are incurable like your blood pressure and diabetes. You have to monitor and control them within the permissible limits. You can't eliminate them. They may be your companions for life. You can neither forget them nor ignore them.

Identify Comparative Advantages These are the advantages that come to you naturally. God has given such advantages to everyone. Blind people are extraordinary in other senses. It is the compensation provided to them knowing the injustice. One should find out what is one's advantage. Somebody did research on the body structure of Michael Phelps and inferred that he has a unique body that is suitable for swimming. That is his comparative advantage.

Forge competitive advantage fair or unfair Only comparative advantage may not be enough. One has to develop it. Leverage it. Phelps spends a minimum of 6 hours in the swimming pool, every day and has a strict diet. Comparative advantage is inherited, and competitive advantages are developed. They are acquired over a period of time through consistent efforts. Some competitive advantages can appear to be unfair to others. Like the advantages developed through social networking or by spending money or compromising values. It is up to the person to decide to what extent he/she should go. Some people feel there is nothing wrong with having or developing unfair advantages, both comparative and competitive when you are competing in an unfair or tough environment. There will always be a flip side, other costs, and trade-offs associated with it. One has to make a choice. All that matters is having a motto --- Just do it.

CHAPTER THIRTY-SIX

Black is not opposite of white

We have a tendency to compare two things and stamp them. This develops prejudice. We unnecessarily treat certain things as opposite, like Black and White. Such prejudice blocks us from looking at the world objectively. Leaders have to develop their perspective to see things as different rather than bad or opposite in nature. (Published on LinkedIn on 13 March 2017. Got 56 Likes; 6 Comments; 5 Shares.)

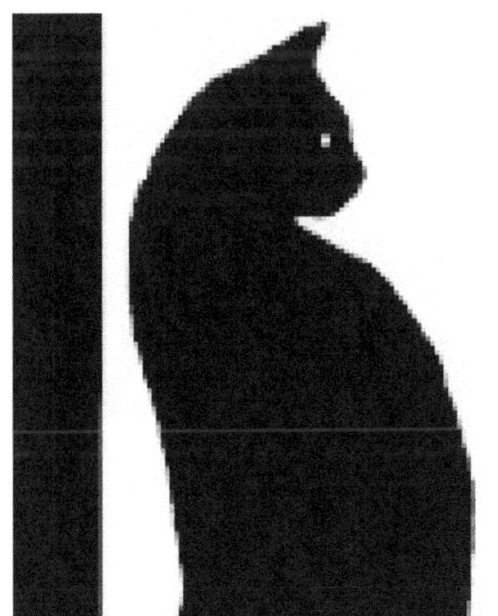

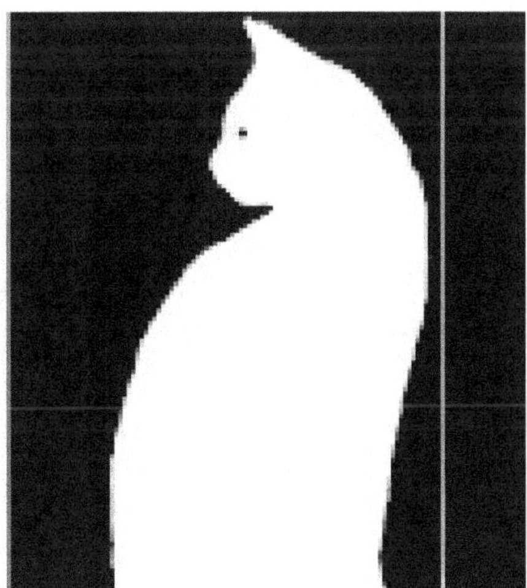

Black is not the opposite of white. Green and red are not opposites. These are only different colours. Sweet and sour are just two different tastes. We believe that if somebody doesn't like sour food, then he should like sweets. Not necessarily. He may like both the tastes or hate them both. Why should dark be the opposite of faint? These are many such funny human interpretations. Such arguments, over a period, shape our perceptions and then the perceptions become a reality.

> *"Inappropriate perceptions develop prejudice. Prejudice can inflict injustice."*

Perception 1: - Look at the picture given on the right side. It is a pencil sketch. The painter has drawn a beautiful scene. He has drawn a small tree, the trunk of a large tree, the ground, some buildings at the end of the field and a lady walking near the trunk of the tree.

Perception 2: - Somebody can develop a perception that it is a pencil sketch of a human face. Look at it carefully with this new perception. To the left of the tree trunk, you can see the face of a man with a clear forehead, eyes nose and lips. This is an example of two different perceptions. Now, these are not opposites. Nothing is right or wrong. They are just two different ways of looking at the same sketch.

> *"Prejudice is the foundation of inequality."*

In my view, there are certain sins which we commit. Those sins result in the wrong perception and hence prejudice. I would like to discuss a few of them:

Labelling and Classifying Humans can't live without names. We label ourselves, our pets, cities, poems, streets, schools everything. Even commodities are labelled to become brands. Labelling is not a just hobby, but it has become our need. We can not stay without labelling. It is the first step toward remembering. The way we remember something depends on the way we label it. Labelling is the function of our perception. If perception is wrong then labelling is wrong. Like in the above example the sketch can be labelled differently & hence remembered differently by different people. Prejudice can spoil labelling. Prejudice is an early judgement which may not be based on reality. We do not stop at labelling. We want to classify things after labelling. We hardly remember unless we classify. After classifying we can relate the label to a particular class and remember it. It is easier to remember such classes by identifying the similarities rather than trying to remember each label separately. But the labels in the same class could be distinctly different from other labels on many other parameters. For example, an Indian can classify Manchurian, Hakka & Cantonese preparations as Chinese food. Travelling in China, you realise cuisines in different parts of China are distinctly different. Southern cuisine is dominated by rice whereas northern is dominated by wheat base preparations. Hakka preparation in the South is radically different from Manchurian cuisine in the northeast of China. The same thing can be true for Punjabi, South Indian and Gujarati preparations. Americans may classify everything as Indian food but as an Indian, your choices could be different. This is the same as having two different perceptions about the above sketch.

Labelling and classifying are the processes by which we create memory hooks

After branding, we want to classify the product as premium or economy. Perception is the foundation of labelling and classification. The wrong perception can create the wrong memory hook. Our behaviour is driven by our memory hooks.

"Prejudice is a wrong memory hook"

People with the right perceptions will behave properly because of the right memory hooks which drive their behaviour. We refer to our labels and classifications as our views or opinions. Once we form opinions, they are tough to change. Just look at the above picture again. Once you label it and classify the sketch as a human face, you do not look at it as a woman walking on the ground near the tree. Even if the painter wanted you to look at it that way (perception 1) you will always look at it differently (perception 2). Moral of the story: we have to be very careful when we do labelling and classifying things initially because we hardly get a second chance to do so.

Gross Generalisation and Simplification To create a memory hook we commit another mistake of gross generalisation. There is a limit to which the human mind can handle variety. Most of the Indian brands had generalised that 'plus size' ladies would not use western wear. A department store chain, Westside, came out with a new western wear brand, Gia, for plus-size ladies by looking at 'in-store videos' which showed such ladies shopping in the gents' section for western outfits. Gia became one of the most successful brands sold by the store chain. Another department store chain took the hint and started a speciality garment chain, in Mumbai, ALL (A Little Large), exclusively for large size customers and doing good business. Department stores were losing out business because of their gross generalisation.

"Generalisation is a process of variety reduction and hence simplification. It is done to create a memory hook"

Obsession with simplification results in gross generalisation. Many times prejudice is the foundation of gross generalisation and oversimplification. For example, the use of words. We try to remember a new word by relating it to synonyms. This is our simplification process which creates a memory hook. But that may not be the right way to learn. For a new person, both smile and laugh mean the same. An example of an oversimplification. For somebody with English as the first language, these words are meant to be used in entirely different situations.

Comparing and saying Good or Bad It is a common disease in humans. When we are served food with different tastes, we tend to say either good or bad. Many things are neither good nor bad they are only different. But we identify a few things which are congruent to our expectations and stamp them as good and others as bad. Sometimes it is exactly the opposite. What we do not have is good and what we have is bad. Ladies with curly hair spent thousands of dollars to make their hair straight. Those with straight hair spent an equal amount to make their hair curly. Dark-skinned people spend a lot of skin whitening creams, and treatments and whites do sunbathe to tan their skin to look dark. What we have is bad and what we do not have is good.

Self-inflicted Prejudice The worst form of prejudice can be self-inflicted. I realised that the world is based on a binary system. It is either 'Present' (1) or 'Absent' (0). In a few cases, we say something is good if it is '1' and bad if it is '0'. It is either present or absent. You are black, or you are not black. You are blond, or you are not. Nothing is good or bad.

"If you have '1' in something, then you will have '0' in something else. The universe is balanced."

Computers are developed with this base of '0' & '1' which is either presence of a current or the absence of it. This combination of '0' & '1' is called byte. Many such bytes make MB and GB. Only '0' or only '1' couldn't have made computers a reality. We need both. Moral of the story: do not worry about your '0's, what you do not have. It is nothing but self-inflicted prejudice. Focus on your '1', what you have. That is a reality.

Second Opinion

When we are facing a grave situation, physical, mental or otherwise, we seek the opinions and advice of experts in the respective field. Sometimes we find it difficult to digest that opinion or advice. We seek advice from another expert. This second opinion either confirms the first or goes against it. Leaders handle this process and their advice well. (Published on LinkedIn on 13 November 2015. Got 16 Likes; 2 Comments and 10 Shares)

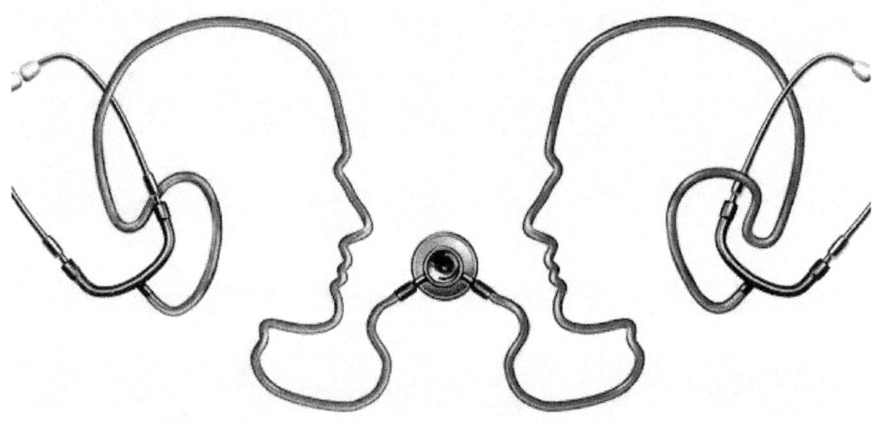

Decision-making is all about taking a qualified judgement and making a choice. The roots of the science of decision-making are found in the judiciary. It provided a framework, tools and processes for making quality decisions. Judiciary is also credited for the important tool- case study analysis, which is widely used in medicine and business management. Western Business schools have been using it as a cutting-edge tool in training business leaders.

Second Opinion

'Second opinion' is very common in the field of medicine. It has its roots in the judiciary. One can always go to the High Court or in rare cases to the Supreme Court after the lower courts deliver their verdict. I always wondered why we doubt their judgement. Judges and doctors take an objective view based on factual reports, tests and evidence. They refer to hundreds of similar cases before delivering a verdict or sharing a diagnosis. They go through the scientific decision-making process. In the business management field, we hardly go for a second opinion. How are the decision-making processes in the corporate world?

Optimum Solution: Focus of the Corporate World

The decision-making in the corporate world is based on: empirical data analysis, simulation, and experimentation. These tools support entrepreneurial gut feelings in the process of making decisions. The focus is on transforming total risk into calculated risk. The business world uses an iterative process of decision-making. Developing various alternatives and then evaluating each alternative for the optimum value. The process is continued till an optimal solution is reached. The optimal solution is always a function of certain variables which depend on the internal and external environment. With changes in certain critical variables the optimal solution changes to sub-optimal. The management then starts formulating and evaluating other alternatives for optimality. This is an ongoing process in every professional business enterprise. Once the decision is made then there is no question of seeking a second opinion. The attempt is made to do it right during the first and the last time. The flip side of the decision is well known and accounted for.

The decision-making process in business management is usually a collective responsibility though the onus is with the leader. It is based on sound processes and data. The jury system of the judiciary has some resemblance. But the juries are not trained, professionals. Most of them lack past experience in judicial judgment-making.

Management of 'Trading Off'

The optimal solution differs from the maximum value solution. Maximum value less value which is traded-off equals optimum value. 'Trade-off' is the critical element in management decision-making. It is a must to take care of friction which might be created due to the maximum value decision. Friction can be the result of opportunity cost, human reactions and psychological cost, long-term interest, investments required, implementation difficulty etc. Trading-off is a talent and skill too. What to trade-off, when, against what are the critical areas of judgement? It requires training and experience besides talent. Management education revolves around developing ability and skill to trade-offs. Focus is on what we are choosing but extreme care is taken to analyse what are we losing, leaving it on the table. Exclusions are analysed more than inclusions. This analysis is in terms of the cost, ramifications, opportunity cost, investments and human elements. Common trade-offs relate to profit versus growth, short-term versus long-term interest, task versus people, performance versus discipline etc. Decision-making in business management is usually a collective opinion process. More than one person is involved in it. Doctors usually make diagnoses without consultations. Except for the jury system, judges also make decisions single-handedly. Is the lack of consultations the foundation of the second opinion? If yes, then there is room to re-engineer the decision-making process in medicine and the judiciary. In a country like India, thousands of cases are pending in courts. It takes at least a couple of decades to deliver justice. Courts are doing sincere and fair work but the system of judiciary needs an overhaul. India can think of going for the jury-based judiciary and restricting most of the cases only to single courts. Otherwise, delayed justice is perceived as injustice.

Multiple Interpretation and Second Opinion

Some argue that the second opinion is necessary because of the chances of multiple interpretations. In my opinion, multiple interpretations is an outcome of a lack of clarity. When the problem and the context are properly defined better clarity can be achieved.

Value Conflict and Second Opinion

The important assumption in the need to eliminate the second opinion is the integrity of the decision maker. If that is doubted then such re-engineering can go for a toss. How do you guarantee integrity during a second opinion? There is room for value conflict at all levels or else why are many country heads serving sentences or being tried in the court of law? The integrity of the decision maker is a separate issue and should not be mixed with the need for a second opinion.

Faith, Belief and Second Opinion

Need to seek a second opinion arises out of a lack of belief and faith. Let us not forget that God heals while the doctor treats. Courts pass judgement but the God gives justice.

CHAPTER THIRTY-EIGHT

Leadership by Partnership

In modern organizations, leadership is evolving. There could be different leaders for different goals depending upon the nature of the goal and the expertise available. Some organizations are testing leadership by rotation so that many people will get benefits and the conceptual skills, cooperation, and coordination within the team improve. (Published on LinkedIn on 4 September 2016. Got 32 Likes; 4 comments and 11 Shares).

In countries like India where the demographics have been dominated by youngsters, the leadership is evolving. The leadership theories, concepts, and practices are required to change in the context of changing the profile of the followers. Gone are the days of followers who blindly obey the leadership. Today, the leadership, in a service economy, has to be radically different than the leadership in the manufacturing economy. Work study concepts like 'standard time', and 'method study' have gone on for a long. Supervision-driven management practices are being replaced by ownership-driven accountability. Employees want higher participation in management. They want an accountable leader who is one among them.

"The emergence of the service economy is accompanied by the emergence of new demographics."

Factors like younger nation, growing middle class, rapid urbanization, changing social order from caste to class, nuclear families with single children and working women at the workplace, etc. are changing the leadership game.

Leadership by Relevance Today, the young generation doesn't accept anybody at the face value. Followers have a questioning mind. Leaders can not sleep on their past laurels. They have to be active, alert, and relevant in the changing scenario or they become extinct. Be it social media or technology, leaders are required to be up to date. Peon, steno-secretaries vanish from Indian offices. Seniors type their own emails and get photocopies themselves. Personal Assistants (PA) are replaced by Executive Assistants who are not just clerks but bright MBA who are being groomed for future leadership.

Leadership by Rotation Today leaders are seen as senior partners. Organizations are getting flatter. Structures are collapsing. Leaders lead partners rather than subordinates. The young generation expects leaders to be hands-on. They want to see the leader doing similar tasks while leading the team. Followers do not want to see leaders doing just administrative work or supervision. The sales team expects a leader to chase key accounts for business rather than just supervision on other salespersons. A coding team expects its leader to develop critical codes.

In sports, a captain has to secure his place on the merits as a player rather than just a captain. Professors expect their students to enjoy Dean's lecture. They want to read research papers written by their Dean. He can't be doing just academic administration.

"The team wants to see the superior DNA of their leader through his work."

I won't be surprised if the trend comes for the 'leadership by rotation' whereby the different members of the team lead the team, at different times. Most of the members of the team become leaders, for some time and lead the team. After their turn, they hand over the baton to other colleagues and become active partners. When managements are expecting employees to take ownership they need employees who have leadership abilities. Leadership by rotation fits the bill and can deliver the results.

Leadership by Example My students are very comfortable with the teaching style which focuses on giving examples. I have observed this generation loves to see examples. They also have a strong sense of equality hence they want leaders to lead by example. They hate leadership with double standards. I have seen young eyebrows getting raised when the tea is served to seniors in a premium crockery set.

"Equality and modesty are important values of the new generation."

Young employees are very upright and love to keep things straight. They love transparency and a fair approach. They want their leader friendly and approachable. They do not want him to be a super-human. He should be rather like an elder sibling with whom they can share and at times develop sibling rivalry. They will only accept leaders who are young in minds and with whom they do not have a generation gap. Youngsters want their leaders to be counselors who provide options rather than trying to push them towards an ideal solution.

Leadership from Non-Striker's End ' Nonstriker' is a partner in a cricket match while batting. He is mostly the unsung hero. Every great inning played by most of the batsmen was always supported by a partner who stood firm on the non-striking end and provided required support, advice, motivation, positive criticism, partnership, and guidance.

"The young generation wants their leader to be like a non-striker with whom they can develop partnerships and deliver results for their organization."

The most interesting facet of such leadership is getting on to the field, supporting the key batsman from the non-striker's end, developing the non-striker's perspective, and leading by developing partnership. For scoring a century a batsman needs moral, professional, emotional, physical, and statistical support. While developing great innings the key batsman has to focus on the game hence he might miss certain non-core aspects. Due to the excitement, he might vibrate emotionally. He wants a partner who is more than just a sounding board. He wants to confirm his gut feel about the changing behavior of the pitch, likely strategy of the competing team, tactics adopted by the bowlers, gaps in the fielding, etc.

"A nonstriking batsman is the 'online support' provided by a team to the player."

A leader is like a non-striker, plays many roles. He is a statistician who provides required numbers and reminds the employee/batsman of important records, he is a leader who leads the performer to victory, and he is a partner who has to score runs himself and contribute positively towards building a big score. When the non-striker starts scoring the batsman gets respite physically and emotionally. The non-striker is the communication channel between the 'dugout' or the dressing room and the batsman, the leader is the communication channel between investors and employees, he is the captain on the field at the winning moment, and he gets the best view of both batting and bowling.

The non-striker promotes singles and double runs while the batsman is busy hitting boundaries and sixes and hence keeps the scoreboard ticking, maintaining the required average. Singles and doubles scored by corporate leaders upset the fielding side/competitors and put constraints on them. Non-striker reminds batsman, constantly, to play to the plan; so does the corporate leader who ensures that the actions are in line with the strategy. The non-striker calms down the batsman when he gets worked up by the slagging done by the opposition. Similarly, a leader responds to the unfair business practice of the competitors. Tomorrow's corporate leaders have to understand these emerging challenges in the field of leadership. I strongly feel that start-ups can handle the young generation better than established organizations. They share a common aspect.... being young. Meanwhile, management researchers should restart their research on leadership..... they need to redefine the leadership wisdom.....all '-isms' are now '-wasms'.

CHAPTER THIRTY-NINE

Collaborating While Competing

Rivalry isn't always bad. It keeps the leadership on toes. But collaboration with the rival is also necessary. The article discusses how to compete but still collaborate. (Published on LinkedIn on 26 July 2017; It got 61 Likes and 7 Comments).

I was a marketing and business development consultant for an organization. Recently, the sales director of the company was complaining about the rivalry between his key employees in the sales team. He was seeking advice on how to avoid such rivalry. He wanted me to counsel them. I rather counseled him,

> *"Rivalry is steam, if managed well, it can run the engine of growth."*

Inability to manage rivalry can ruin the structure of the organization and weaken the foundation. A rivalry is a competition for the same objective or for superiority in the same field. When employees compete with their peers for achieving organizational objectives then the 'performance culture' prevails in the organization.

> *"A rivalry develops a commitment to the cause. A rivalry develops a passion for the purpose."*

Unless the person is driven strongly by some objective and he/she is very keen to achieve it, he/she doesn't develop a rivalry. Rivalry indicates a person's desperation to achieve something. The leader must understand the desperation of his team members. The rivalry will provide a lot of insights to the leader. He would know why the person is working. what motives him? He can manage the team better if he knows the purpose and the motives of the team members.

> *"The leader has to connect rivalry to the mission."*

Once the team competes for the mission then the organization gets into the jet speed track. The rivalry is like the useful bacteria in curd (yogurt), Lactobacillus bulgaricus. They help in digestion by breaking the proteins which are difficult to digest by the human gut. The leadership skill is to develop rivalry like curd and use it to the benefit of the team. When an employee develops an ego in his Key Result Areas (KRA) then his commitment level goes up. He knows that he can over power others only by achieving his KRA.

"Competition in the marketplace requires competition in the workplace."

The competitive spirit is the fuel that ignites the performance. It is potential energy. The team leader has to apply a performance pressure to convert it to kinetic energy. The employee should know if he /she doesn't rise to the occasion, somebody else will. A rivalry develops a hunger for business. Such hunger drives business.

"Rivalry keeps employees alert. Lack of rivalry develops monopoly and monotony."

When an employee knows only he can do the job, then he develops arrogance. He develops monopolistic behavior. When many people are competent, then there is a tussle between them to get the job. Only the best must be given the job. It improves the quality and the productivity of work, which is good for the customers & the employer. A rivalry develops specialists. Employees try to develop knowledge and learn skills that can help them out-performing others.

"Too much job security is detrimental to the growth of the employee. Rivalry is usually associated with insecurity."

Government employees enjoy excessive job security. How many of them make efforts to update the required knowledge & skills? How does that job security help the employer and the customers/citizens?

"Rivalry can be a boon if it triggers healthy competition."

It is difficult to define 'healthy competition'. When the returns and rewards are directly proportionate to the talent, eligibility, experience (qualitative and quantitative), sacrifice, and contribution of the employee then we can say that the competition is fair. The Key to the success is collaborating while competing I grew up at my native place, Solapur, in Maharashtra state of Western India. It is a drought-prone area and had no employment opportunities. We could develop our careers only through bright academic performances and migrate to fortunate cities like Mumbai or Pune for career advancement. In my childhood, I observed that in some families, all siblings did well in their careers. What could be the reason? The elder siblings performed in their careers, they created peer pressure. Sibling rivalry was generated. But the elder siblings supported the younger ones. They provided the required guidance. While parents were too busy to look into the studies of their kids, the elder siblings guided their younger brothers/ sisters in studies. They collaborated with younger siblings and performed the role of the parents. While competing they created collaborations. Their primary objective was to bring laurels to the family and make parents proud. As a result, sibling collaborations combined with sibling rivalry, the younger siblings out-performed their elder siblings. They made their families proud. They created the city brand. Corporate leaders could emulate similar family cultures in their teams. They have to create collaborations. They have to groom sibling rivalry. They have to ensure the team members complement each other while they compete with each other. They have to facilitate communication, and cooperation between competing employees and competing teams. We can find many applications for this approach. In a Coalition government, political parties with different agendas work together. They compete in their constituencies during elections. But post elections they have to collaborate with competing parties to form the government. They complement their coalition partners to deliver results or else they face defeat in the next elections. For the last three years, India had a President and Prime Minister from competing parties which are arch rivals. But they worked together in harmony demonstrating political maturity. They demonstrated to the world why India is not only the largest but the greatest democracy in the world. They taught a lesson or two to a few developed countries. They showed how to complement, how to collaborate with competitors for the national cause. It was like Dick Cheney collaborating with Hilary. Indian politicians have acquired this skill while their counterparts in Japan and Italy struggled to collaborate, making unstable governments. India had many federal and state coalition governments in the past and hardly a few collapsed on account of political rivalry. Such coalition governments completing the entire five-year term is the hallmark of the Indian democracy. Sales teams are like coalition governments. They have to form teams with competitors. They have to support their internal competitors. They know the individual performance can go down unless the team performs. They will be losers if the team loses, irrespective of their personal sales performance. They can climb only on the backs of their rivals.

"A salesperson dances with the competitors but ensures that he keeps a step ahead or else he crushes his toe."

Trump's Problem President Donald Trump is struggling to collaborate while he competes with China, India, and Mexico. He must understand this principle well. He has to compete with China, prove his superiority, and create manufacturing jobs in America. But he must collaborate with China for the national cause. He has to use his clever mind prudently to decide the right mix of 'make or buy'. One may have tall claims but the fact is China is America's factory. America depends on Mexico for the supply of labor. But for such support, America will be like Japan, which is struggling because of the lack of a labor force. Visionary American political and business leaders have consciously developed that business model. Though American economy is certainly experiencing the heat of the flip side. Even Indians can't deny that Americans are losing their jobs to cheap outsourcing. These countries must collaborate to settle differences. They can fight but they have to dance together. President Xi Jing Ping demonstrates that maturity and the world expect the same from President Trump. Earlier he transforms the Chinese rivalry into sibling rivalry, happier will be the world.

Why do such collaborations with the competitors work? Such collaborations with the competitors work because they create synergy. The energy source gets doubled because of the collaboration.

What It Takes What are the special qualities required to successfully collaborate with rivals? There is no check list but one can identify some personal qualities required. Some of those qualities are--

- Passion for the objective, target, or power.
- Fair Self Evaluation of one's strengths and weaknesses.
- Faith in the partnership Knowing partner's strength and ability to add value.
- The conceptual ability involves an ability to look at the total picture and maintain patience and tolerance till the final picture gets right.
- Belief in collective wisdom. Accept the decision even if you don't agree.
- Openness to being reviewed or criticized, Ability to work with talented people;
- Be it the President or the government or companies or individuals, the ability to collaborate with the competitor while competing with him can change the future for the better.

www.ingramcontent.com/pod-product-compliance
Lightning Source LLC
Chambersburg PA
CBHW071411150726
48000CB00001B/262